Daisy and Bob: Letters, 1939-44

A Love Story of World War II

Transcribed and Edited by Nikki Guy Latham

Daisy and Bob: Letters, 1939-44
A Love Story of World War II

Transcribed and Edited by Nikki Guy Latham

Copyright ©2020 Nikki Guy Latham

ISBN 978-0-578-28669-3 print
ISBN 978-0-578-28670-9 ePub

All rights reserved. No part of this publication may be reproduced, distributed, or transmitted in any form or by any means, including photocopying, recording, or other electronic or mechanical methods, without the prior written permission of the publisher, except in the case of brief quotations embodied in critical reviews and certain other noncommercial uses permitted by copyright law.

Book design by StoriesToTellBooks.com

Daisy and Bob: Letters, 1939-44

A Love Story of World War II

Contents

Introduction	*vii*
Family and Friends	*ix*
I. 1939—Daisy	1
II. 1940—Daisy and Bob	26
III. 1941—Married Life	101
IV. 1942—Baby Makes Three	114
V. 1943—Far from Home	150
VI. 1944—The Price of Freedom	188
Epilogue	*227*

To the Soldiers,
and Those who Love Them

"I was trying to make sense out of it."
[film, Extremely Loud and Incredibly Close, Directed by Stephen Daidry, Warner Bros. 2011, Blu-ray, DVD, digital download]

Daisy and Nikki

To Daisy
January, 1944
Italy

Hey My Dearest Darling,

...You have been doing an excellent job in sticking by me. Your letters are all that a man could ask for, and knowing that you and Nikki are waiting for me makes this life bearable...

I am looking forward to that day when I get off the train in Chester and rush to meet you...

All my love forever,
Bob

Introduction

It's 1944. In an old photo, I'm a chubby toddler, wearing a snow suit, and standing outside with my mother Daisy. I'm squinting at the winter sun. She wears a fur coat and a brimmed hat. With one hand, she holds my hand; with the other, a cigarette. She's twenty-one. My father Bob, twenty-five, is not in the picture. As a U.S. Army officer in World War II, he has been overseas for eight months, and is now "somewhere in Italy." Their only communication is by letter; they write to each other almost daily.

Love grows in letters. Longing does too. Most of my parents' courtship was by letters. Bob worked for a year in New York, and Daisy attended the University of South Carolina. Telephone calls, telegrams, and visits were too expensive for them, just out of the Depression. They married on December 7, 1940, after Bob enlisted in the U. S. Army. Frequently apart again, due to Bob's Army training, they continued to write.

I was born on November 4, 1942. Despite many protests and dire warnings of her relatives, Mother carried me in a basket on the long trip to El Paso, Texas, to be with my father. I was six-weeks-old. She often talked about the stress of that journey: the crowded troop trains, the dirty bathrooms where she mixed my formula. Our family had three months together, until Bob, an Army lieutenant, shipped out to the battles of World War II in North Africa.

The first time I knew about their letters was when I was twelve. Exploring our large furniture-filled attic, I found and read two of the letters. They seemed "mushy," and probably off-limits to me. I put them back in the small cedar box.

After Mother died at age 88, my younger sister gave me four large boxes of their letters from the attic. I have copied and minimally edited them.

In reading the letters, it's as if I can, for the first time, hear them talking to each other, and saying they love me too, their baby.

~Nikki Guy Latham

Family and Friends

- Daisy ("Sister")
- Bob
- Daisy's Parents: John Nixon (Nick) and Daisy Hampton
- Her Brothers: Kirk, 18 years older than Daisy, wife Harriet, children Patti and Kirkwood; John ("Stuff"), 12 years older than Daisy, wife Mary
- Best friend: Isabel
- His Parents: R. C. Sr. and stepmother Alice
- His Brothers: James, wife Sally; R. C. Jr., wife Mamie
- His Sisters: Eleanor, Virginia, Ann Davis ("Da Da," pronounced Day Day)
- Many Chester friends, couples they knew in the Army, and comrades-in-arms.

All the letters we have, starting in the summer of 1939, were written by Daisy; Bob must have saved them. She was 17; he was 21. She met him a year earlier when she went to church with Isabel, Bob's cousin. While still in high school, she went out with Bob on weekends. Bob graduated from Clemson, and left for summer ROTC Camp in Edgewood Arsenal, Maryland, on June 9, 1939.

Daisy

Bob

I. 1939—Daisy

June 20, 1939
Greenville, SC

Hey My Darling,

Bob, I'm in the most awful fix. I'm lonesome for the first time in my life and I don't know what to do about it. I go to a picture show and lose track of what it's about. I read and don't know what's on the page I just read. People talk to me, and sometimes I don't hear them. I've been going out at night. When the boy I'm with says something to me, half the time I don't know what he's saying. I laugh and cut the fool and try to make some bright remarks and wonder why I went out with him when I had rather be by myself if I can't be with the only person in the world I'll ever love, you... I read your letter 6 times.

Darling, please remember I love you... I'm putting my heart down on paper cause I can't tell you in person and I don't want you to forget.

All my Love, Daisy

June 22, 1939
Greenville

Hope it is cooler where you are than here... Well, Sweet, I had all my hair cut off today and the ends curled. It looks 100% better, and feels equally as good... There are three cases of polio in Chester. Your last letter was wonderful. I felt exactly as if you were talking to me.

It helped so much... I wish I could have spent yesterday with you. Know why? It was the longest day of the year. Oh well, we'll spend a lot of them together someday... Darling, Patti has asked me several nights if you were coming to see me. It made me feel so funny inside when I told her no. Remember the boy I had a date with Friday night? I saw him over the weekend and went to the picture show with him to see "There Goes My Heart. " It was a real good show. I decided then I didn't want to date him anymore and I haven't. He was awfully nice to me but I thought about you the whole time, so what was the use of going out with him?

There's a party tomorrow for a girl who's getting married; this afternoon I'm going to see "The Next Time I Marry. " I still wake up during the night thinking that you are holding me in your arms. . . I love you—much & much, more & more, forever and ever.

July 3, 1939
Chester, SC

Hey My Darling,

Received your letter today and enjoyed it so much I decided to write you again! . . . You sound sort of down in the dumps. Please don't feel that way—there isn't the slightest doubt in my mind that you will be anything but a success. . . I'm going to be terribly proud of you always. I'm going to the Creek with Isabel for the 4th, but will feel funny that you are not with me. I'm sad that you're so far away, but I don't show it to anybody. I'm not interested in the boys around here. . . I support your plan to work in New York.

Bob, I want to see you so bad tonight it hurts. Darling, I will keep your heart and love you forever. . .

July 7, 1939
Chester

Hey My Darling,

I would have loved to see you Monday but guess it's all for the best you didn't come, 'cause you would have had to leave almost before you got here. . . Cousin Lizzie asked what I was doing without you.

Darling, Papa's tobacco is beautiful, it's blooming and it's real even. Isabel and I had a picnic in the dining room on the Fourth: fried chicken, chicken salad, pickles, cake, iced tea, paper plates & cups. We sat on the steps going upstairs like we did last summer...

Red gave Margaret a beautiful engagement ring, and has built a house for her at Clinton. When a storm woke me up last night, I was dreaming about you. This morning, I cut out and basted a dress. My friend ____ surprised everyone by marrying the doctor she was going with. Mother said she knows I'm in love with you and will marry you. I denied it, but I know it will come true.

All My Love to You, Daisy

July 18, 1939
Chester

Hey My Darling,

I'm glad you are having such a good time. Darling, I don't think I would be much of a person if I didn't want the man I love to have a good time.

Pete (W.) thinks that you'll meet someone else, or I will. He thinks we are so far away from each other that it won't last. He thinks that you have to be with a person all the time and kissing them to know that you love them... Bob, it makes me feel so good to know that our love isn't cheap and is going to last always. I tried to explain to Pete that if he was in love, he wouldn't even want to be with anyone else. He said he was ready to get married so I told him he had better be sure he's in love...

Isabel's in Florence; she had a date with a Jr at the Citadel, and they sure had fun! I spent Friday night in town and saw "Masie". Darling, this is the longest summer, & I have two more months before I leave for Greenwood to go to Lander College... I miss you so dam much. I love you lots & lots, loads & loads, and HEAPS & HEAPS...

[*After completing R. O. T. C. camp, Bob is working with Ciba Company in New York City.*]

July 22, 1939
Chester

Hey My Darling,

Received your letter today so I just had to write. Mother said, "So you can't resist writing as soon as you hear from that Boy." She thinks I ought to write you every other week and let it go at that. She thought when you went to New York we'd wish each other well and say good-by but she just doesn't know I wouldn't do that for the whole world.

Isabel and I went to Lowrys yesterday and got caught in a bad storm coming back from the orchard. We stopped at Byre's Station and bought cheese crackers, olives, potato chips and candy. Darling it was raining and I couldn't help but think of all the times we've been together when it poured down. Bob, I wanted you to hold me in your arms... We came home, crawled out of the window to the porch and had a picnic. We had a grand time sitting on an old trunk eating and smoking. I talked so much I got right hoarse... I know you're thrilled about working in New York... I know you'll be a success. I'll always be pulling for you 'cause I love you so much. You'll be a regular Yankee 'fore you know it...

Went to the Show with Pete, Dodge and Harriet. We rode in the back of a pick-up truck... Pete said you probably would work a few years and meet someone else... I'm not afraid, 'cause we're meant for each other...

Daisy

Aug 1, 1939
Chester

Hey My Darling,

Walking down the path, I read your letter. Bob, I would love to be waiting for you when you come home from work, more than anything else in the world...

Isabel (S.) is ready to marry Pete (Wy.) as soon as he asks her. I don't know how they can afford it... I am finally allowed to wear black, and I got a cute dress... It's a beautiful night outside; I feel close to you because we had so many beautiful nights with the moon shining last summer before you left... Nick wants me to go two years to Lander, then to Carolina. Do I need a PhD to qualify to be your wife? I miss you just as much as the day you left. All my love and a long goodnight kiss.

Daisy

Aug 1, 1939
Chester

Hey My Darling,

I watched the moon on Saturday night and missed you. Kirk wanted to know if we writing each other. Bob, it seems as if everyone but you, myself & Isabel thinks that our romance is very passé. Can you hear frogs croaking at night? I imagine you hear cars, trains, buses and trucks, etc.

Pete's always saying or doing the things that remind him of you, for my benefit. If he only knew I don't have to be reminded not one bit 'cause I always feel as if you are a part of me and are always near. He sang "Turn Off the Moon" the other night 'cause he said you and he used to sing it to two sisters, the summer 'fore last during peach season.

With all my love always,

Daisy

Aug 2, 1939
Chester

Hey My Darling,

Your letter to-day is one of the sweetest letters you've ever written me. Don't ever stop telling me how much you love me 'cause it thrills me just as much, or more, than the first time you told me at the Pond. Remember how terribly happy I was that night? I'll never forget how I felt. Darling, I love you when you're sentimental ('bout me). In fact I love you lots & lots, loads & loads and heaps & heaps, in any mood.

You all seem to have a very nice apartment. Do you all have a stove?

(She encloses a clipping about an excellent peach season at the Lowrys orchards.)

Aug. 11, 1939
Chester

Hey My Darling,

Isabel Wy. and Pete are so happy. He told me he wouldn't be single again for anything in the world. . . Her wedding ring is gold with tiny little diamonds across the front. It looks somewhat like the ring Grandmother gave me. I wish you could see them. . . Neither family said one word of objection. Pete said he thought Mrs. S. was going to have a heart attack but she was very pleasant. Her father thanked him, and they welcomed him as part of the family. Darling your letter was so sweet I felt like crying, I wanted to be in your arms so bad. The part about us being married was so beautiful. I've read that part about 50 times, and it thrills me every time. We'll make it come true someday. Darling, I hate that ole 'someday'. Let's don't say it anymore. . .

Listen, Darling, please don't be jealous of Pete or anyone else 'cause other people simply do not count. Bob, you're the only boy I've ever wanted to marry and live with the rest of my life. See Darling, I love you, only you. I don't even think about anyone else; can't, 'cause I'm thinking 'bout you all the time. When I read your letter, I felt exactly as if you were holding me in your arms, talking in my ear... Darling, I'm so scared there might be a war. That would be terrible...

I close with all my love for you always, Daisy

Aug 15, 1939
Chester

I saw a darling little light-haired girl to-day with her hair rolled up in curlers! Bob, I don't think we'll roll any of our little girls' hair up in curlers. I like them better just like they are... I was tickled to find I had three long letters from you. Darling, some of your letters sound as if you don't really believe I love you. As if I met someone else, I wouldn't love you anymore, or not as much as I do now. Don't you know that I can't love anyone else, there just isn't any room left in my heart. You have it all. I love you and will keep on loving you. If you once start loving someone you can't stop. Bob, other people just don't exist as far as I'm concerned. Don't you know I'd do anything in the world to be able to go to sleep every night in your arms, and wake up knowing that I really belonged to you? Darling, please don't ever call it quits unless you mean it. I want to wait for you; loving you makes the time pass faster. You said something about not writing so often. I want you to write me for pleasure, not a duty. I'll love you even more after two years. Nick has a swell new tobacco barn with oil burners. The tobacco is so pretty growing in the fields...

Isabel and I say that you will make a good husband because you're thoughtful. I wish you were working in Greenville, isn't that selfish? I can't help it. I do. I'm glad you like my letters; I want to kiss you a million times... Mother thinks I'm much too young to be in love. Pete took me out to the Pond where we used to go. I saw two shooting stars and missed you so much; I felt like part of me was missing.

Aug 16, 1939
Chester

[She sent him a Song Sheet and wants to hear him sing "I Love You Truly".]
In later years, Daisy said that Bob was rejected in a New York singing audition, because he looked and sounded too much like Bing Crosby to be a success.

Aug 19, 1939
Chester

Glad to hear you are seeing some people from home... I served Mother breakfast in bed since she wasn't feeling well, washed dishes, did the housecleaning and sewing...

Aug 21, 1939
Chester

Nearly three months since you left and seems like three long years... I want you to be very positive about marrying me...

This past year at school, when I knew that you were coming home on Friday or Saturday, I couldn't do a thing that whole week 'cause I was thinking 'bout you... Then I was excited over seeing you and couldn't do a thing the next week. When I'd get a letter from you, I wouldn't even hear a word in class... Thank goodness, High School is over... If you were working nearby, I couldn't go off to school...

Aug 22, 1939
Chester

Hey My Darling,

Isabel and I bought wedding presents for Isabel and Pete Wy. They have their marriage license stuck in the side of the mirror and Pete said he gets up and reads it every morning just so he'll know he isn't dreaming... Isabel Wy. is so settled now and wants to save every penny. Much to my surprise, Daisy & Nick said they thought it is a good thing they got married.

This is the longest summer I've ever been through... Keep on loving me Darling.

Aug 24, 1939
Chester

Well, Darling, I don't think your future wife (If I'm it) will go to college... Kirk wants me to live with them in Greenville and go to Business School with Sissy [a relative], so I'd be able to do something. He can get me a job in Greenville when I finish and, furthermore, he didn't see much use in my "wasting" two years at Lander, although it was nice to say you'd been to college. He said if I was really set on going I could. But I realize that Nick's not getting any younger and it would be a strain on him, and if anything happened to him, I certainly wouldn't feel like living off of Kirk...

Bob, I'm scared to death you might have to go to war. I don't know what I'd do then. It's bad enough you being so far away but at least I know you're alright...

Aug 26, 1939
Chester

How do you like you all's new apartment? It sounds real nice. Bob, I will adore going apartment hunting with you. Don't you think we'd go for something real cozy and home-like?

My last date's drinking and getting sick embarrassed me a lot. I didn't want to go out tonight.

They're picking cotton now. I see a tiny little boy, who lives in that house behind us, and looks too small to walk, going to the field, with a little cotton picking sack over his shoulder, with his mother...

You're the only one I write; I wish you were still at Clemson.

Aug 29, 1939
Chester

... Isabel doesn't want to go to Winthrop, but to Business School in Washington... It sure looks as if Germany put Japan in a tight spot, by selling them out to Russia, doesn't it?

On August 23, 1939, Nazi Germany and the Soviet Union signed a non-aggression pact. Japan had relied on Germany to defend Japanese interests against Russia in China and Asia.
~Chicago Daily Tribune, 8/23/1939

Aug 30, 1939
Chester

I enjoyed your letter, and want to be with you. I refused a date; someday I'll have a date with you every single night... Nick searched for his new white-faced bull for 4 days, then found him in a corner of the pasture...

Aug 31, 1939
Chester

I miss you and feel like crying, like that day at the Creek when I knew you were going so far away. I can hardly wait 'til we will be together always. I saw "Stronger Than Desire" at the picture show. Isabel and Bill aren't going together—it wasn't love because they never did understand each other... I think that we understand each other pretty well... I hope you like New York more than ever 'cause it helps knowing you are satisfied with everything...

On September 1, 1939, Nazi Germany invaded Poland, the act that started World War II. France and England declared war on Germany September 3, but neither country was prepared to fight, and would not deploy a significant number of military forces until the next year. On September 17, the Soviet Red Army invaded Poland from the east. The last organized Polish resistance was defeated on October 6. Although things appeared to quiet down, German forces steadily occupied Poland, and continued to focus on civilians, imprisoning and murdering thousands of the country's residents.
~The Learning Network, New York Times, 9/1/2011

Sept 2, 1939
Chester

Hey My Darling,

I love the picture. It's real good of you. It made me want to be with you so bad. You sound so ambitious and I'm so proud of you. Dad came in this afternoon and told me Germany has started fighting those poor Poles... Darling, I'm so scared you're going to have to go I don't know what to do... that would be terrible. I never realized how Mother felt about war and how Harriet won't even let Kirk say anything about it until now. I never thought much about war, but it's different when you love someone with all your soul and body, as I do you. It's hell to think about it.

Sept 9, 1939
Chester

I kiss your picture at night. Enjoyed your letter so much. Darling, I'm so scared about the war. I just didn't believe they would ever start fighting and when England joined up that just brought it closer home, and to top it all, you're going to Camp this coming summer. It makes me feel so helpless and scared. I guess I am sort of helpless but I hate to think I am.

Isabel and Pete Wy. are so happy fixing up their new home. Some of our other friends have eloped—the rings are very pretty. I am going to college because Nick wants me to have at least a year of school. He said that Isabel and I were 'just babies and should look up the word "marriage" in the dictionary.'... We went shopping, and tried on hats. I bargained for one and got my price.

We went to see "Lady of the Tropics. " It was sad. They showed a newsreel of Poland & England and some of the fighting and it's awful... I miss you, having trouble going to sleep. I'm sorry I didn't write a letter for Monday, after you said you wanted one. I love you every minute of the day.

Bob don't you dare ever let me hear you thinking or talking 'bout entering the Army for active service. Darling, I don't want to be a widow; I don't want to be scared out of my wits half the time I'm married to you, wondering if there's going to be war and where you'll be. If you were fighting, every night I'd see you dead lying in the mud. Darling isn't that awful. I couldn't stand it. You're crazy 'bout your work and New York so please don't think 'bout joining the Army.

I'm planning to go to the University of South Carolina, and stay at the new Dormitory... It's beautiful with lovely wallpaper, built-in desks, several closets, a tile bath between every room, and hardwood floors. Study hall is at the end of each hall, grand with soft rubber matting... there's a special trunk room... When Nick & I went in the Dean's office and told her his last name, the Dean's assistant wanted to know if he was Stuff's [brother John] Daddy! Bob, I'm going to love college. Nick and I are so thrilled, he said he'd like to go back! He showed me where he roomed and Harriet's father roomed in the building across the way... Nick and I even watched the boys practicing football. They're huge... Had a grand dinner of soft-shelled crabs and all the trimmings, then we went to the picture show. Well, Darling, guess you're glad I'm going to college. Didn't you say you were old-fashioned about your wife going to school. Nick's pulling for 4 years at school but I don't know. I love the looks of the place. I'll write lots when I get there. I leave the 18th. Darling, when we're married, I'm going to take good care of you and make you take the cold serum every year. Bob please take care of yourself.

Love Always, Daisy

Sept 15, 1939
Chester

Darling, I don't feel tied to you. Didn't you tell me one night when we were sitting out front of my house that you didn't ever expect to stop going out with girls 'till you got married? I love you Darling. I enjoyed your letter... I always want you to tell me exactly how you feel in your heart.

Bob, I'm so scared all the time about your going to war, and last night, I woke up all of a sudden with the most awful feeling that I'd just been told you were going. I couldn't get back to sleep for ages, and Darling I wanted you to hold me close so bad...

Stuff came to see us and had about a bushel of snapshots of grand-looking girls in bathing suits, that he went out with at the Beach. Isabel went to Winthrop on Monday, didn't want to go, and doesn't like her roommates. Harriet D. said I'm not the type to be a secretary... I won't ever fall in love with anyone but you.

I don't like you being so far away... I think America will declare war in a year's time, if not sooner... We've been going together two years now, and I haven't seen you in three months.

Sept 19, 1939
Columbia, SC

Mother and I went shopping this morning and I got a grand looking black dress for nice. It's made out of some new stuff and has two aqua clips on each side of the neck. Got a black sweater and skirt. I bought two pretty spreads, rose and blue tufted, and a blue and rose Comfort. Got some other things, but doubt if you'd be interested. I always said that if I ever got out of Chester High, I'd never go to any school again. Funny how things work out, isn't it? My one main ambition in life is marriage and children.

Nick says I can't come home till Xmas! He says he & Daisy

Hampton will really enjoy being by themselves this winter and there'll be no silly talk!

One of my friends had to leave Winthrop for sneaking out at night...

Isabel Wy. is getting another ring and their house is real cute.

[In September, 1939, Daisy became a student at the University of South Carolina, Columbia. Isabel went to Winthrop College in Rock Hill, S. C.]

Sept 22, 1939
Columbia

Got your letter to-day and that's the first time I've felt like I wanted to cry and cry since I've been here... My roommate is red-headed and my height. She's swell, and I'm crazy about her... We went to ride with some boys we met at the Drug Store. I met a girl who knew you at Clemson and said you were a good dancer... We've been standing all kinds of horrid old tests...

Sept 25, 1939
Columbia

Hey My Darling,

Your letters were grand... My roommate is so sweet... We have 3 big closets, with shoe racks, beautiful wallpaper, twin beds, cute bedside tables, Venetian shades, tile bath, just everything you can think of. I love it down here; classes start tomorrow. I dreamed about you, and don't mind if you snore. You'd be swell to live with. It must be hard to save money in NY or any big city. I'm terribly glad we didn't go too far with each other, even though we wanted to. I adore wearing your [fraternity] pin, and your love is worth a dozen rings. I miss your kisses so much... I'm going across the hall now, to play poker with some girls...

Sept 27, 1939

Hey My Dear Darling,

After I read your letter today... I just lay across my bed and cried... There are loads of cute people here, but they just make me want to be with you twice as bad. No one will ever take your place. I'd rather you see my real feelings than anyone else. You're so sweet writing me so often. It makes me feel so good knowing that you love me and always will...

Down here, we do exactly as we please—smoke in class and eat with the boys, or anywhere we want. Even if I don't see you this Christmas, I look forward to other Christmases with our children.

Oct 2, 1939

A crowd of us started talking about war last night. The Dean says America will go to war within six months. I pray that he is wrong... I sure wish you weren't in the R. O. T. C...

Oct 5, 1939

I wish I could have been with you when you were feeling so lonesome. I want you to hold me, and I miss you especially at night... I bought a blue Angora sweater, a light pink one and a blue skirt. Stuff sends me money, and I have $10 allowance from Dad, and extra as needed. I feel very rich... I saw 'Naughty but Nice', and "Golden Boy." I hate Gym; we play some silly game called bad mitten that has a ball with feathers on it. You have to hit the dam thing so hard to get it across the net, but I guess it's good for me.

Gosh, more girls here are getting married soon. . . I look forward to hearing from you about our future together. . . Please don't drink too much. It will hurt me after we're married if I ever see you drunk. . .

All My Love, Daisy

Oct 11, 1939

I think it's grand you all get 4 days for Thanksgiving. Sure wish you could come home but don't imagine you can. Please take care of yourself. Don't you think you ought to see about your tooth? I went out with some girls to a swanky part of town last night. We had good food and played lots of records. . . I'm only existing while I'm so far from you. Seems like years since you've kissed me. I'm proud that you're living a clean life, and glad you get to hear so many grand orchestras. . .

Oct 20, 1939
Columbia

I saw Clemson win. . . Darling, don't try to suppress the desire you have for me, it doesn't help much I know, 'cause I've tried. . . and it's always there stronger than ever, just as if I'd never tried. Bob, I'm glad we want each other, it's one of the things that makes me so sure that we are meant for each other even if it is hard now, I know it's all for the best, but I have such a restless nature. We'll be together "someday. " I'm going to Charleston Saturday with Amy for a wedding and to the beach – Nick and Daisy don't know I'm going. . . After a dance last Sat. , we had a mild wreck, and didn't get back until 1:00. . .

Oct. 24, 1939
Columbia

Amy and I went to the Citadel; those boys were nice to us. I dated a junior, who's assistant manager of the football team. I don't care a doodle about him, but he was nice. . . I want to be with you all the time. . .

Oct 26, 1939
Columbia

Hey My Dear Darling,

Bob, are you ever lonesome? I am, even with all the people that are here. I want to be alone with you. . . Isabel is coming for the weekend. I wish you were too, but not here, with no privacy. . . I had my physical by a young doctor who dates a senior; he told another girl that my skin was 'so white.' . .

All My Love Always, Daisy

Oct 31, 1939
Columbia

I'm glad you went to Washington. . . Isabel hates Winthrop . . .

I miss home. The rain tonight reminds me of the times we were together. . .

Nov 6, 1939
Columbia

Hey My Dear Darling,

I enjoyed your letter. . . I want to wake up in the night, feel you lying close, and know there aren't any barriers, that we really belong to each other. You will make me more than happy. It's wonderful that James and Sally are going to have a baby. . . You won't make me wait long, will you?. . . I saw "The Old Maid," and "Lady of the Tropics."

Darling, I send my love to you for always and always, Daisy

Nov. 10, 1939
Columbia

I was in the college infirmary with flu . . . Darling, I miss you so much and it's only been 5 months, which seems like years, what are the next three or four years going to seem like? Centuries, I imagine. . .

Nov 13, 1939
Columbia

I enjoyed your letter as always. . . Mother & Daddy came to see me Saturday and took Amy and I out to dinner, and Daddy went on to the game to see Furman—we went to the show because I wouldn't sit out in the wind after having the flu. Mother looked grand, she was all fixed-up and Daddy had the time of his life meeting all those girls. You would have thought he was 20 the way he acted. I wish you were coming home Thanksgiving or Christmas. I've seen you every Christmas before, but only one Thanksgiving. . .

Nov 17, 1939
Columbia

I'm well now, but the second night in the infirmary, they wouldn't let anybody visit me. But after the lights were out, three football players, who were hurt, came on back anyway. Miss Long caught them, and put them back to bed...

I miss you... I'm glad you had a good time with Eleanor... I'll go home for Thanksgiving, but would rather be with you.

Nov 19, 1939
Columbia

Hey My Dear Darling,

Bob, I'd love to come up every time I wanted to, but I'm afraid you can't afford "us" yet... I wish I could have been with you when you walked down by the river. Saw "Drums Along the Mohawk" yesterday. It's a grand picture except for the fighting. The girls across the hall are teaching me to play bridge. Darling, I hope you spent a happy Thanksgiving in Washington. Sometimes I get so restless I don't know what to do. Everything I do just seems to lack something. It's you.

All My Love Always, Daisy

Nov 24, 1939
Chester, SC

I sure was thrilled this morning when you sent me an airmail, that's the first time you've ever done that. Darling, I enjoyed what you said in both your letters... I came home from school on the bus, saw friends, had a date, and visited with Kirk and his family. Harriet wanted to know if I liked any of the boys at Carolina better than I do you. Guess what I told her—I never would. How's that? Darling, I love you so much and wish you were here so bad 'til it's awful. Darling, I wish I could go to sleep in your arms every night.

Nov 27, 1939
Columbia

Hey My Dearest Darling,

I want to be with you so bad. . . Last Thanksgiving night we were in Greenville; it was cold, and raining just like it is here now. Darling, every time I write New York on the front of one of my letters to you it makes me right sick. I know I shouldn't feel that way, but sometimes I just can't help it. Isabel and I went to Charlotte yesterday, and bought a girdle apiece. We're just too fat. Stuff wrote me I had better not gain any more weight. . . I enjoyed myself more the last time I was in Charlotte, with you. . . I had another date with Pete last night . . . We went by Mr. E. G. 's, got his new car, and then went down to Mack's. . . I took the first drink without a chaser and they thought I was crazy 'cause I didn't even make a face. We got a bottle of white grape wine, but I didn't have a good time. . . Daisy & Nick still think of me as their baby. I am, but I thought they'd at least think I am a little older. . . Every time I went out, Nick said "Sister, don't stay out too late!" My favorite song, "My Prayer," is playing right now. Nick couldn't stand it any longer; he got a radio so he could listen to all the football games. Dr. Croner made my braces tight today. . . Darling I'm so glad Eleanor and Virginia are driving up, 'cause you'll have somebody there. That helps so much. . .

Nov 29, 1939
Columbia

I'm glad you spent Thanksgiving in Washington. . . Darling, we'll have a grand time making a home together. . . It was so sweet of you to write me the night you got back, even though you were sleepy. . . I want to be with you for the rest of my life. . .

Nov 30, 1939
Columbia

... I would love to have you hold me in your arms 'til dawn... Our friends here haven't changed a bit... Listen, Darling. don't you ever say or write the word jealous again... You're the only one I'll ever love... I am yours. I feel as if I'm really married to you and you've just gone away for a while; no one can take your place... Don't worry about me; I'm as happy as I'll ever be without you.

Dec 1, 1939
Columbia

Your letter was a sweet surprise... Four of us went to see "Remember," and it was grand... You can hardly take a step without bumping into a soldier on the streets of Columbia. I hate the way some of 'em look at you. A man from Camden, I used to write to, came by the house—he's a first lieutenant, and wants to take me to an officers' supper. I think he's crazy to want to take out someone as young as I am.

Dec 4, 1939
Columbia

Enjoyed your letter so much. Darling, I love the part about dedicating the rest of your life to me. I tell you what—we'll dedicate our lives to each other... If you proposed in person, I wouldn't let you back out on me!

I want to come and see you for Christmas, and hope R. C. can give me a ride...

Dec 6, 1939
Columbia

I want to be married to you, and not have to say, "Don't..."
My roommate spends all her time chasing a football player...

Dec 8, 1939
Columbia

Darling I have to see you. Even if I have to catch the train, Darling, I'm determined to see you Christmas. It's been much too long since you held me close... I played bridge until late last night...

We passed the matron's room inspection by shoving everything in the closet and under the bed... I look forward to seeing you in Washington for Christmas...

Dec 14, 1939
Columbia

I'm thrilled so terribly much over the idea of seeing you in only a few days. Darling, it's almost too good to be true—to be in your arms again. I can hardly wait... Dada [Bob's sister] wrote me the sweetest letter and asked me to stay with her. It made me feel so good 'cause I wasn't expecting her to write me. I know it will be different there, and your folks will want to see you a lot, but I don't mind... I'm worried about your having so many colds. Please take cold shots, be careful, and don't get the flu.

Dec. 27, 1939
Chester

Good Morning My Darling,

I missed you not waking me up this morning. Someday you can wake me up every morning. . . Bob, I had such a grand time. It was the best Christmas I've ever spent. Just being with you. Darling, I love your family. They seem to have so much fun together. Darling, please forgive me for the way I acted about what you told me. Darling, I'm glad you told me because I know you love me. It was just that I'd never thought of anything like that before and when you told me it sort of knocked the props out from under me. When I'd shut my eyes, I could see you with your arms around somebody else like I'd wanted to be a million times. I just couldn't talk. . . Darling I can't ever stop loving you I don't care what happens. It's just there and every time you take me in your arms, I nearly go crazy. Darling, I love the House Coat, so does Mother; even Daddy thought it felt good. I love you always, your Daisy

II. 1940—Daisy and Bob

Daisy attended college and business school for most of 1940. Bob worked in New York.

"If you find my lover, tell him I am weak with love."

~Song of Songs 5:8

Jan 1, 1940
Chester

Hey My Darling,

Thanks a million for the telegram. Nick went to the phone and said he'd take it! He had more fun over that; Daddy likes you. He wouldn't give me your letter until after I had fixed dessert. He said to tell you to stay in New York until I finish school! Do you remember how weak I was when I stood up beside you early Monday morning? I've never felt so happy... I got a permanent wave; it doesn't look so hot... Pete gave Isabel an engagement ring with 3 diamonds in it. I feel so dam let down after being with you. Part of me is missing. I love you so much for always. Nothing can ever change that...

Jan 3, 1940
Columbia

Well, I leave for school to-night. I was ready to go back as soon as I left you Monday night at the station. I felt awful, seeing you go. I missed you so dam much New Year's Eve. I went out with Pete W., Harriet and Hoover; got in at 4:00... Did you go down to "Times Square?" I heard the program on the radio...

Jan. 5, 1940
Columbia

Our love will last over the years. It's not possible for me to love anyone else... Yes, I listen to Glenn Miller but I wouldn't know his orchestra from any other if the announcer didn't tell me who it was. Darling, I'm still scared about the U. S. going into war. I have the strangest feeling every time I think about it. Oh My Darling, that would be terrible... We had a wonderful time together at Christmas... My friends love the housecoat you gave me...

By January 1940, Germany and Russia have divided Poland, and the Nazis have begun to euthanize the sick and disabled in Germany. To increase their military bases, Soviet forces invaded Finland, at which time the USSR was expelled from the United Nations. Meanwhile, both Britain and Germany were moving ships in convoys, laying minefields, sinking ships, and using depth charges to destroy submarines. Rationing has begun in Britain.

Jan 9,1940
Columbia

Your letter was swell, and I don't want you to be afraid that I don't love you, and will forever... I know exactly how you felt, because I felt that way all last summer after you left. Nearly every day I expected a letter from you saying you didn't love me anymore... I want to marry you and no one else.

I'm thinking about going with Amy to work in summer stock in Virginia.

I'm not sure if my parents would like it. Amy said it would help me see reality, and not always through "rose-colored glasses".

Jan 10, 1940
Columbia

When you take me in your arms I get as weak as water, and I feel so happy and completely satisfied being near you...

Jan 12, 1940
Columbia

We had ice on Sunday at school; the power went out and the girls were screaming, laughing, and running around the halls—it was more fun. I want to room with Amy next semester... I heard a loud yell down the hall last night; a girl had come in with a huge engagement ring that was a surprise; they plan to marry in June... It seems so long until we will get married...

Jan 19, 1940
Columbia

I love the mood you were in when you wrote me. It made me feel so close to you, and that everything isn't so far away and hopeless as it seemed. Christmas morning seems like a wonderful dream...

Jan 20, 1940
Columbia

It snowed this morning; pretty, but cold... I wish you could be my roommate. Twin beds, like we have in the rooms, would be a complete washout when you're terribly, desperately and passionately in love, as I am with you... I dreamed we were married and had a baby...

Jan 25, 1940
Chester, SC

I love you loads and loads, lots and lots and heaps and heaps... Chester had 6 inches of snow. Nick & Kirk are cussing...

I'm having a hard time with History—but I studied and

passed. I didn't want to tell Nick I flunked... I miss you, and I'm just putting in time at school.

Jan 27, 1940
Chester

I got a letter and some money from Stuff to-day... Went in Miss Hattie's Bookstore; she said to thank you for your Christmas card. Mother and Dad went to see "Swanee River. " I'm looking forward to seeing you next summer...

Jan 29, 1940
Chester

On Saturday, Isabel and a crowd of us went in the back of the Standard Pharmacy and drank wine; we went to two parties. I didn't like my date... I miss you...

Jan 30, 1940
Columbia

Hey My Dearest Darling,

I felt so good when I found a letter waiting for me here, and such a swell one too. I love the way you tell me you love me. Bob, I was scared to look at my marks, 'cause I haven't done a dam thing this semester. I didn't hand in 3 themes for English, and I've busted every English quiz we've had since mid-semester. I just can't do grammar, and that's what our exam was on. He gave me a C for the semester. I think that's wonderful for the little bit of effort I put forth, and all the cuts I've taken... After you go off to school, when you go home you feel as if you don't belong there. I didn't see how on earth Nick and Daisy would get along without me but I think they get along much better. They enjoy being by themselves, 'cause I'm so much younger than they are. Mother has always said I am more of a granddaughter than a daughter. She spoils Nick more than ever and he seems to love it.

Isabel said she had tough luck with her love affairs, but she's glad she had something to do with bringing us together. I am too, but Darling I think we'd have met sooner or later... I think you'd make a wonderful husband right now. You suit me fine...

Jan 31, 1940
Columbia

I want you to keep saying 'I love you,' and I would like to live in NY, or anywhere with you. I spend 99% of my spare time daydreaming about when we'll be together... Nick thinks Isabel and I are too young to know whether we're in love. But Mother was my age when she married him...

Feb 1, 1940
Columbia

Darling, sometimes I'm afraid you're lonesome, not having anyone you care about with you. When I can be with you, I'll make sure you're not lonesome... I want you to tell me what I need to do to be a good wife.

Feb 3, 1940
Columbia

I won .46 ¢ and a hamburger last night playing poker... I convinced the dean to change my roommate to Amy... I'm glad you got a raise, but I'd like to be there, kiss you every morning, and fix your breakfast... I like your writing about "our baby."

Feb 7, 1940
Columbia

Stuff called to-night; Daddy's been very sick and has a nurse with him.

He told me to come home this weekend, but I'm going Thursday Night. I'm scared... Daddy's letter said he wasn't feeling good...

Feb 8, 1940
Columbia

Daddy's a lot better... Your letter was grand... I don't want a fancy wedding, just you. No one else can take your place. The dean said they couldn't keep up with the girls, or where they spent the night—two got married last night, and they had rarely slept in the dormitory. I didn't realize such girls existed...

Feb 9, 1940
Chester

Hey My Dearest Darling, Dad had a heart attack Sunday afternoon. Kirk and Harriet got here about 9 Sunday night and Stuff came down right away and has been here since then...

Daddy is not to do any work. He'll be in bed for about 5 or 6 weeks. Everybody has been coming out and doing things... I've been sitting by the bed, holding his hand & talking to him. I can hardly keep from crying. He knows what he had and told me all about it. I got supper to-night and fed him. He can't even sit up. The Doctor only lets him smoke a few cigs. He tries to fool his nurse about how many. Darling, I wish you could be here with me. Mother's been so hurt over the whole thing, that I wouldn't let her see me cry... Darling, I love you so much, I wish I could go to sleep every night in your arms...

Feb 13, 1940
Columbia

I'm back at school! Don't guess I can say prison, for it's anything but! I wonder what it's going to be like not to count the hours I can spend with you, to know I have every right to be with you day and night as your wife. I know it's going to be heaven. I don't even think money counts. When I'm with you, money seems so unimportant. Isabel's learning to jitterbug! From now on, she, says, the man she goes out with will have some money. "Money, not love" is her motto! I don't think it'll work 'cause what good will money do when you don't love the person?

Feb 14, 1940
Columbia

Reading your letters makes me want to be with you so bad. It's awful to know we can't for a long time. Please don't even think about giving me a diamond ring. . . All I want is your love, and a plain wedding band. I like to talk a lot when I get up in the morning, but if you don't feel like talking, I'll try not to bother you. Gosh, I bet you're going to be provoked as hell at me lots of times, especially when I'm in one of my silly moods. . . If I ever get in one of those strange moods, as I was on Christmas morning, just grab me and keep kissing me just as hard as you can. 'Cause I can't resist when you kiss me that way.

Feb 15, 1940
Columbia

Bob, I loved your telegram. The man sang it to me. Thanks Darling.

Heard from Mother today and she says Nick's doing what they tell him. I sent him a big red heart box of candy... I think if anything should happen to Nick, it would just about kill me. I know I'd have to get over it but I wouldn't ever want to go home again...

I enjoyed your letter so much yesterday. You're right about not really understanding each other until we have a child. That sounds grand, doesn't it? There isn't a night that I don't wish I were in your arms... I didn't go to bed until 3:00 this morning—I was finishing up my scrap book for Interior Decorating. Only 3 others finished theirs...

Feb 18, 1940
Columbia

Your letter was so sweet... Amy and I went to see "Gone with the Wind"... It was wonderful. Rhett Butler was grand. Gosh, when he carried her upstairs that night, I don't think he was as drunk as he made out. She sure had a satisfied look on her face the next morning. Darling, I know I'm going to be just that satisfied, or more, the next morning after our first night together. I love you...

Feb 20, 1940
Columbia

Sometimes I wonder if we'll ever be together for always; sometimes I'm afraid... I just know one thing: I'll always love you no matter what happens even if you told me you were going to marry someone else...

Feb 22, 1940
Columbia

Hey My Dearest Darling,

I've been sleeping without clothes and it's so comfortable . . . Amy and I went to see "A Child is Born. " It's a good picture, but terribly sad. I cried so much. . . I understand why you can't marry me now, and I can wait as long as you want to, even 4 years. . .

I'm not used to having much, and can do without. . .

Feb 25, 1940
Columbia

Christmas seems as if it were a wonderful dream. I felt as if I really belonged to you that night on the sofa. Darling, I know we are meant for each other, but sometimes it seems so far away. . . Went out with Stuff & Coach to the Columbia Hotel; 4 salesmen joined us in drinking Scotch & Soda. We had dinner, went to the boxing matches and had a grand time. Stuff wants to get me a job this summer in Concord. He said I shouldn't think about getting married yet because I haven't been around enough people. Maybe he's right. . .

March 2, 1940
Columbia

Hey My Dearest Darling,

I feel ashamed of what I wrote since I read your letter today. You made me feel exactly as if I am a child and have done something I shouldn't. Darling, I'm so sorry. If you'd blessed me out, I wouldn't have felt so bad about saying that to you, but when you turn around and write me a sweet letter, Darling, I can't do a thing but love you that much more. I was scared to hear from you 'cause I just knew you were going to tell me where to go and you had every right to do so. Bob, if you ever want to do anything, no matter what it is, I want you to go ahead 'cause I'm not going to stand in your way. I have no right whatsoever to object to anything. I made that mistake once, and I don't want to make it again. In other words, if you told me you were going to California to work, I'd say "That's nice, Bob. "... No matter what you do, I'll always love you and will always want to be your wife. I think you're right about learning a lot about life from someone you like. You've taught me just about everything I know and made me realize that I have emotions that I never dreamed I had. Darling, I'm glad you have taught me. I didn't feel well, cut 5 classes, and will go home for the weekend. I love you lots & lots, Loads & Loads & heaps & Heaps. Always will.

March 4, 1940
Columbia

Well, I'm back... Mrs. M. came out yesterday and I went back to town with her. Henry & I went to ride. You all must really have a wonderful time in New York. He told me about the time you went to sleep, and he tried to take your shoes off. New York must be wonderful with no one telling you what to do. I can't see why any of you would want to come South, ever. Amy & I are going to Lancaster this weekend, and are expecting to do every crazy thing we want. If I feel the way I do now, I'm going to get tight as hell. It's a good thing that we've decided not to say anything to each other about what we do. The girl we're going to see likes to raise hell and drink. They generally go to Great Falls to some of the Honkey Tonks...

My love for always, Daisy.

Bob, I think we should stop talking about getting married 'cause everything is so uncertain.

March 5, 1940
Chester

I'm at home, sitting by Nick's bed: we're listening to the Carolina-Duke game. When I come home, I always think you should be here to come see me...

Guess what, Darling, I'm turning over a new leaf. I'm actually going to church tomorrow... That's one thing we'll do after we're married. Harriet sent Nick a darling picture of little Kirkwood. It must be wonderful to have a baby and know you had him because you loved someone very much. Oh, Darling, I wish we were married. I don't know why you put up with me, I'm so impatient... I'm scared you're going to have to go to war. It seems to be crowding in from all sides. Nick said to tell you he wasn't doing well, and he can't have anything he wants.

In February 1940, the British government called for volunteers to fight in Finland, but Finland surrendered to the USSR in March. Hitler ordered unrestricted submarine warfare, and directed his generals to plan the invasion of Denmark and Norway. The U. S., recovering from the Depression, was not yet involved in the war.

March 7, 1940
Columbia

Hey My Dearest Darling,

I was scared to hear from you to-day because I must have hurt you by my letter. I've felt so bad ever since. It's the first time in my whole life I've ever really cared what someone thought of me. It matters more than anything what you think of me... If I could just be with you for 10 min., and tell you how sorry I am.

Darling, I've got to learn to give in easier than I do; I don't want you to be the one who gives in all the time—you'd learn to hate me, and I never want that to happen. You don't have to forgive me this time, or even write if you don't feel like it. I wouldn't blame you if you didn't. I'll always love you. Daisy

March 8, 1940
Columbia

Your letter made me feel so funny. I felt as if I'd been going with you several weeks and you had written me just a nice letter. I know that's the type of letter I deserve, but I don't like it. Darling, please, love me like you used to. I never thought I'd say that to any man, because I've always had too much pride.

Bob, I don't have a dam bit of pride where you're concerned, and I'd do anything to make you feel as you did before I wrote you those awful letters. I've never felt tied to you, wish I was. I've been scared that you feel you are tied to me. Darling, I'll never want any other man like I want you. . . I feel so bad about how much I've hurt you. I don't want to go anywhere this weekend but home to Nick. I feel so dam young. It's not much fun to go home anymore and see him sick. If you decide you'd rather not write me anymore, I'll understand. . . I'll never stop loving you as long as I live.

March 9, 1940
Columbia

All that's happened, and how scared I've been, has made me realize how terrible it would be if I lost you. When you said in your letter today that maybe I was right, that you'd stop talking about getting married, it made me realize you were going to say that you didn't love me. Darling, I'll wait as long as you want me to... I couldn't think of being married to anyone but you, or anyone touching me as you have. You've never made me feel tied to you and you aren't one bit jealous...

March 12, 1940
Columbia

Went with Amy to Lancaster—her cousin got us dates with older men who are rich and don't work. Mine said I acted like I was in love with someone else, and that was foolish. I got mad and didn't like him at all... I'll keep my chin up and pull for you as long as you want me to. Bob, I know you're going to be a success.

March 14, 1940
Columbia

I love you... you're wonderful. You're too dam sweet to me...

I enjoyed your airmail so much. If you told me you didn't love me anymore, it would have been all my fault. I had hurt you too. Darling, I feel as if I really belong to you... Mother said they are going to let Nick sit up, but she's still scared...

March 19, 1940
Columbia

I'm tired of your being so far away, and you're not coming home till July! That's ages away, but I still love you with all my heart and always will... If you go to Camp in Atlanta, I'm going there too! I do believe in you no matter how far away you are. It's wonderful to want somebody and know they want you just as bad.

March 20, 1940
Columbia

I'm going to Charleston tomorrow with a girl who has a car... Well, Darling, how does it feel to be a whole year older?

Remember you came home on the weekend of your last birthday and went somewhere with C. that night. It's funny to think how mad I was & couldn't say a dam word... You sound lonesome for the South...

March 27, 1940
Yonges Island, SC

It's wonderful down here. We've been to the beach 3 times. Last night T. came about 8, and we got home at 2. He reminds me so much of you. We went on a chicken fry, and there was a good bit of drinking. I would take a glass and split it with him. He wants to kiss a lot, but I miss you. We went boat riding... I enjoyed your letters so much. Thanks for writing me here... Darling, I want to be with you every day and night. I've obviously made up my mind that I'm not going to marry you until I'm sure you're ready...

March 29, 1940
Columbia

I went to the beach, and was asked out by many boys (one from the Citadel). I've been dancing and having fun... I love you Darling, Me

April 1, 1940
Columbia

Hey My Dear, Dear Darling,

I have not heard from you in 3 days. Have you been sick? That scares me when I don't hear from you. Darling, I miss you so dam much all the time. I wish I was living with you in New York. I know we'd have a grand time just being together. In one of your letters, you said something about our lives molding together, and that not everything can run smooth all the time. I know that, but the way we love each other, everything will work out. There are going to be plenty of times when I will have to give in to you. I hate to give in, but I'm willing to do anything if it makes you happy. Mary, John's wife, said it's been grand weather for flying, especially at night. Can't you see Dad's face when he hears that?

April 2, 1940
Columbia

Dear Bob,

Are you sick? Are you just paying me back for not writing you? Or what? I haven't heard from you in 4 days. Have you decided not to write me anymore? I would like to know. Love Always, Daisy

April 3, 1940
Columbia

Just finished reading your letter. Darling, I'm sorry I told you about kissing somebody else. I didn't think for one min. that you cared whether I did or not. Strange, I thought you said a man feels different about things. Do you think I enjoyed being kissed by somebody else? I've never said anything about your kissing anyone 'cause I know you do. Please don't be jealous; you're the only man I'll ever love. Maybe it would have been better if we hadn't met until after you came back from New York, but we wouldn't know each other like we do now. I've tried to stop loving you, because we can't get married for a long time... I'm sorry I've said all I did. I'm willing to wait several years if you want to...

April 4, 1940
Columbia

Hey My Dearest Darling, Bob,

I want to be with you so bad to-night, and you're so far away. I was disappointed when I read that you didn't think you'd be home till Aug., and then you wouldn't be at camp right outside of Atlanta, but 110 miles away.

April 5, 1940
Columbia

I love you so much and I'm so sorry about those people I kissed Easter. I didn't do anything else and never will except when I'm in your arms... How is your work? Are you under a new boss? I think they should send you South. We didn't know how lucky we were last year seeing each other on the weekends...

April 6, 1940
Columbia

Bob,

I'm so sorry about the extra week but I'm glad you told me now 'cause I couldn't have stood waiting and expecting you, and at the last minute finding out you weren't coming. Darling, we can't expect things to come our way all the time, and have to make the most of them when they do. One week will not be so much, when we're going to spend the rest of our lives together. I love you so much that one week won't make me stop. Everything is bound to work out. I think you're right to go to Camp this summer and get it over with, then next summer you'll have two whole weeks at home. I know we're both disappointed as hell, and you feel terrible. I wish I could be with you for a little while. I'm glad you tell me things; it makes me know you love me. If I write you more would it help? I'm so sorry about only 3 letters in two weeks. Why, that was only 1 ½ letters a week. I'm going to try not to cry and make the best of everything. Summer is a good time off yet and anything can happen between now and then. Please don't worry and, no matter what happens, I'll always be loving you and waiting for you. . .

April 8, 1940
Chester

Hey My Dearest Darling,

Well, I'm home, and I felt so good when I found a letter from you waiting on me. I was expecting it; you generally write me when I come home and it helps so much. I wish I could be with you. I wish I were your wife, and then we wouldn't suffer like we do. . . I'm glad you care what I do but please don't be jealous. . . Just tell me what you expect me to do.

Nick likes to hear Bonnie Baker sing on the radio. Kirkwood has grown so much. He is blond, fat and walking. Kirk looks so proud of his son. Kirk & Harriet are so much in love. . . I got an aqua silk dress and matching coat for $14.50. You should see me in it. . .

1940—Daisy and Bob

April 9, 1940
Chester

Darling,

Thanks so much for inviting me to come see you... I doubt if Nick and Daisy would like me to be alone with you in New York...

Also, I couldn't trust myself... Dad is walking around in the yard, but the Doctor won't let him go very far. He looks real well. He knows I'm in love with you but he's still hoping that I'll decide I'm too young to be in love... Bob, I'm scared 'cause we know war is coming & it's not so far off.

April 10, 1940
Chester

I'm so glad you feel better now. Why didn't you ask me to write you more? B. married Kathleen H. Mattie and Doug are married. Mary married a boy that works in some grocery store at home. Isabel Wy. gets up at 5:30, gives Pete breakfast & gets him to work! She still says married life is wonderful. Darling, you're right about waiting two or three more years to get married. Everything is so unsettled, and America is bound to go to war in another year. I can wait on the man I love, and can't imagine living with anyone but you. I understand that you have to wait until you are surer of things, and living in New York is anything but cheap. Why Bob, if I were living there, I'd be afraid to go out by myself 'cause I know I'd get lost. You like N. Y. so much and your job, so it won't hurt us to wait three years anyway. Why, some people wait 10...

In April 1940, the Germans took the city of Oslo, Norway, and occupied Copenhagen, Denmark. Although the U.S. was not in the war, President Roosevelt made preparations to re-arm America, and to support Great Britain in their war efforts.

April 11, 1940
Columbia

I read your letter today; when you said how blue you were, Darling, I wanted to be with you so bad. It's an awful feeling to be restless and can't find the right thing to do. I never felt that way until I fell in love with you. It doesn't matter how long we have to wait, because everything will be all right after we are married, and we're young now. Sometimes, you sound discouraged. Please don't be, things are bound to come our way before long. The Campus is pretty now, with trees and grass a deep green, and flowers blooming. It's warm and everyone is wearing thin clothes. I wish I could be with you when you feel blue, put my arms around your neck, kiss you long and hard, and tell you how much I love you.

April 12, 1940
Columbia

I'm restless and nervous as hell tonight. I've smoked a whole pkg. of Pall Mall since this afternoon. Everything I do falls flat and nothing seems to satisfy me. I just want you to reach out, grab me, kiss me, and never let me go.

April 15, 1940
Columbia

I miss you so much. Always do. You seem so far away. This is when I hate Ciba and everything that keeps me away from you. I hate all this waiting and I'm scared stiff about war coming along...

When I tell you how I feel, it gives me the best feeling. It seems so natural to tell you things that I wouldn't dare tell, even Mother. I'm going home tomorrow afternoon because no one stays here on the week-ends. Let's don't plan on a weekend in Washington quite yet as things are so unsettled. I might be working, and don't know where I'll be...

April 15, 1940
Columbia

Oh, my Darling, your letter made me realize all over again how much I love you and always will. When you tell me that you want to do the right thing, so we'll have a whole lifetime of happiness, it's so much easier. Sometimes I think time makes a lot of things easier. I want to see you before you come home this summer. I've been smoking so much lately, every two or three minutes. I'm not going to smoke after we get married because I think it would be a waste of money. I'm really going to try to make you a good wife. I'm going to try so hard to please you, so you'll always love and want me. We're going to have to do without a lot of things, but it won't hurt us as long as we have each other.

April 18, 1940
Columbia

It's been almost a year since you told me you were going to work in New York. I couldn't live last summer over again for anything. Everything seems so hopeless...

April 25, 1940
Columbia

I wrote you that I wouldn't marry you, but I tore the letter up...

I thought our love had just become a habit, but I still love and want you...

April 25, 1940
Columbia

Hey My Dearest Darling,

We danced in the barn last night. We drove around the countryside, and Nick was mad... We almost had a wreck... I got your letters when I got back. Darling, when you write me like that, I want to be your wife so bad. I don't understand what kind of a mood you were in when you said that after we're married, you want me to humor you. What kind of moods do you have? I've often wondered but never exactly knew. I never can forget you; that would be impossible... I told Nick I wish I could marry you right now. He laughed and said no one would want to marry anyone as silly as I am. He doesn't think I have a serious thought in my head but I do...

April 30, 1940
Columbia

I was thrilled to get your special delivery this morning. I felt weak, as if I was drunk after reading about your love for me... I'm happy and proud; we are meant for each other. I don't want us to lose control with each other before we're married...

May 2, 1940
Columbia

I feel hopeless at night. All my thoughts revolve around you. I can't say anything about your being in New York another year, but that I'll love you wherever you are...

May 4, 1940
Columbia

It's now 2:15 and I've just finished rolling up my hair and putting on my night gown. Sissy and I are writing, and Amy's asleep... I wish I could put my arms around your neck and lie close to you like we did Xmas morning. It must be heaven to be married, when there aren't any barriers to hold you apart... Kirk kissed Harriet four times Saturday night before they went to bed. You should see little Kirkwood smile when Big Kirk picks him up. Patti's a real big girl now. Harriet is going to take her to see "Pinocchio," and she's thrilled to death. I wonder what you're doing now... I hope you're not drinking. If you tell me to mind my own business, I'm going to say, "Well whose business is it, if it isn't mine!"

May 7, 1940
Columbia

Darling, our outlook isn't so bad. You have a good job and you'll get along fine. I don't mind waiting on the man I love... Maude B. wrote that a child with extra drawings reminded her so much of me. Isn't this grand—a real little girl in Designing class poked out her finger to me today with a lovely engagement ring! They have been going together 10 months, have saved $250, and when she finishes school, they'll have $1,000 in the Bank. He is only the associate manager at a Picture Show! Bob, I thought you write to other girls. Remember, you told me you were writing to 5 at one time... I hope to see you in Washington...

May 9, 1940
Columbia

Hey My Dearest Darling,

I finished reading your letter, and Darling, you sound so depressed. Bob, you must not be; it won't help matters one bit. Just about this time last year you were all thrilled over going to New York, and now you're there. I can't come to Washington; Mother says it would look as if I were running after you. . .

I want you to have a good time and not worry about saving money. . .

May 17, 1940
Columbia

I want to be with you the whole night when you're home. . . I'm not sure how late I can stay out; I don't want to upset my father. . .

June 4, 1940
Chester

It was hell for me when I saw the train pull out. I enjoyed being with you so much this past weekend. I have never been as happy in my whole life. It was so much fun fixing lunch and going visiting together. I love you more because you show respect for my wishes. Mother and Dad are listening to the war news. Nick says he would join up if he was 30 years younger. . . He likes you a lot. Listen, Darling. Please take care of yourself and gain some weight. Please try to get a little more sleep. . . You have all my love, and will forever. . . It seems so natural to tell you things. Sometimes I'm so afraid we aren't going to lead our life together because of this awful war. If war breaks out, I'm going to live with you before you go. . .

June 8, 1940
Chester

I'm glad James [Bob's brother] and Sally had a boy—James was probably scared it would be a girl. . . War scares me because it will ruin our lives; Nick says it's coming for sure. . . Jane [Isabel's mother] said all of Lowrys knew about our activities on your visit.

On May 10, Germany invaded Belgium, France, Luxembourg and the Netherlands.
Winston Churchill, the new British prime Minister, said, "We are in the preliminary stage of one of the greatest battles in history. . . We are in action at many points. . . We have to be prepared for the Mediterranean. . . The air battle is continuous. . . We have before us many, many long months of struggle and of suffering. . . Without victory, there is no survival. . . "
Churchill asked Roosevelt and Canada for aid. On June 10, Italy declared war on France.

June 12, 1940
Chester

It's pouring down. . . Remember how you used to come and see me when it was pouring?

Hey My Dear Darling,

I love you, I got supper tonight & washed dishes. This time last week, I had seen you off on the train, and was, by now, lying in bed trying to sleep. . . All this weekend I've been thinking of you, pressing me close and kissing me. I liked that you called me 'wife-to-be' in your letter. I dance better with you. . . While your roommates are away, please get some sleep and drink your milk. See, I already sound like your wife.

Italy has declared war on the Allies. I listened to the President's speech. Bob, I'm scared. I just know we aren't going to get to live together. America's bound to go to war and I'm afraid it's going to be within a year. The President now has the power to call out the National Guard. Bob, how will this affect you? Nick says the President will call out the "N. G." in 30 days or less. Darling, it looks as if we're getting all the wrong breaks. I feel so helpless about everything. I used to think when two people wanted to get married, they did. I'm beginning to find out how wrong I am about so many things. I think I'm beginning to grow up. . . It's been so long since you kissed me good-bye at the train. . . Why does this war have to come along and ruin our lives? We don't want war. I don't want you going to war. I want to be your wife and have your children and live quietly with you; now it looks as if our lives are just going to be shattered. It's all so awful and useless. I feel a little hysterical about the whole business. I got up at 6 this morning, got breakfast, and cleaned the house. I cooked dinner, skimmed the cream off the milk & churned and made butter. Mother's been doing some sewing for herself. I had a very busy day but enjoyed it because time passed so fast. I love you always, Daisy

June 14, 1940
Chester

_____'s baby was born dead. She was in a wreck before it was born.

Hey My Dearest Darling Papa,

Hope you spent a happy Father's Day! It's hot as hell here. . . I enjoyed your letter so much, and am glad to hear you're drinking milk. Are you drinking it straight or mixed with gin? You know straight will have much more effect. It looks as if we're headed straight for war. I think the French are going to give up, they just can't hold up... I can't come to Washington because I can't ask Nick for the money. I know he hasn't got it right now. I'm so sorry...

June 20, 1940
Chester

I stayed with Isabel over the weekend. P. got angry because we didn't want to go to the square dance. Have you ever thought that when you go to Camp this summer, the President might station you all somewhere?

June 25, 1940
Chester

I'm going to a lot of weddings... When I wore a full skirt, Nick told me that I looked like 'a ship under full sail.' I would like to give you 20 lbs...

June 26, 1940
Chester

I wish your dream of waking up next to me was true... I wasn't at all surprised when you told me about the letter you got requesting you to volunteer for the Army. I knew it was coming sooner or later. Darling I want you to do what you think is best. Just remember, whatever you do, I'll be pulling for you all the way...

I imagine it's hard to decide. I'm scared that pretty soon they aren't going to ask anyone to volunteer but are going to demand. If war comes, I just want you to be as high up as you can get...

I'm glad your friends are back so you won't be so lonesome. It's been raining here all morning and it's real chilly. Darling, I love you with all my heart and always will.

June 28, 1940
Chester

[Bob has volunteered for the Army]

Hey My Dearest Darling,

Thank you for writing so often. Isabel Wy. is going to have a baby, and is tickled to death. She said it would make their happiness complete. They weren't afraid to get married, and everything worked out fine. They have spunk. . .

I've been wondering how long Great Britain will be able to hold out. . . I think war will come soon. I am getting used to you being in NY, and that there will be many years until we get married, if ever. You have no idea how bad it hurt last year, when I knew you were going away. I wouldn't live over that time for anything in this world. I think soon it's going to be a natural thing to say good-by to you every 6 or 8 months. . . What you did is right. It scared me at first but if war comes, you'll be up that much higher. Nick said you showed good sense. I'm not going to say anything to anyone, because I know you'd rather tell them. Darling, you'll be a success. No matter what you do I'll always love & want you. I'm still hoping to get to Washington but can't let you know until next week. It's sweet of you to want to pay my way but I can't let you do that. Do you have any idea where you'll be stationed? When you go with the Army, does it mean we'll have to wait several more years? I'd live in one room with you and be perfectly happy. . .

July 1, 1940
Chester

I'm afraid Washington is out, Darling. You know I want to be with you but I just can't come. I'm so sorry. I hope you have a good time, and please think of me a little. Will you?

July 16, 1940
Chester

I am keeping house while Mother is in Greenville. Isabel is staying with me. Nick is giving us talks on the good of the Army... Right now, he's got some poor man sitting outside with him, talking war. The man came to see him about cattle. I'm thinking about forgetting you because it's hard to miss you so much... With all my love, Daisy

[*The letters we have from Bob begin here. He is at summer R. O. T. C. camp.*]

Date uncertain
Ft. Benning, Ga.

Hey My Dearest Darling,

This is actually the first time I have stopped since I arrived. Maybe you were right. The Army is going to take up a hell of a lot of time, but Darling don't worry I will certainly find time to write you. Daisy, I sure enjoyed the day I spent with you. Wish it could have been a week or more... It is going to be a hell of a lot of work and a hell of a lot of fun here. I wanted to let you know that I am thinking of you tonight. . . All my love for always, Bob

July 25, 1940
Daisy in Chester

Hey My Dearest Darling,

    I'm sorry to hear that you're kept out in the sun so much. I enjoyed being with you Sat. night. I didn't mind your talking in circles, so terribly much. Darling, I realize that you have no idea what you really want to do, and that your family thinks it would be wrong for you to get married before four or five years at the least. Maybe they are right. I'm glad you told me what you did Sat. night about being scared of marriage. Bob, I think it's better to wait too. I want my marriage the best I can make it, but I can't make it by myself. I'm sorry I said all this but I just had to. I'll always love you with all my heart. No, Darling, I'm not mad at your folks' not calling me. I don't want you to ever do anything you don't want to, where I'm concerned. I guess I did have a good deal of nerve asking you to call me. It's right funny how much one comes to think they mean to a person they love. Please be careful while you're at Camp. I'm always scared that something will blow up or something. . . I miss you more than I can tell. Darling, I've never thought I had you on a string because I've always been afraid you didn't love me, but I do love you with all my heart. Isabel says that we're going to raise hell. I'm not, though; it's not any fun without you.

    P. S. Is the change you're talking about, in circles, your feeling toward me? I want to know right away. I'll understand and not bother you anymore, or say anything. I'll send your [fraternity] pin back. Feels like I am writing to a stranger now. . .

> July 26, 1940
> Daisy in Chester

I'm staying with Isabel... Yesterday we went to the Book Club at your home. We washed up the silver & dishes afterwards for Alice. We visited people and went to see "We Who Are Young". We are going to the Bible School Picnic... What did you think of my letter yesterday? I just have to know whether you care or not...

> July 30, 1940
> Daisy in Chester

Hey My Dearest Darling, I've never been so glad to hear from anyone in all my life. I understand now that you do not have much chance to write, so I won't expect any letters. Your letter made me feel grand. I'm glad you are coming home for the weekend. I want to have a big time and kiss you...

> Aug 8, 1940
> Daisy in Greenville

I enjoyed this past weekend so much. I've lived over Sat. Night a million times in my mind. It was as if I really were yours... Bob, it made me feel good to see you looking so well... Isabel and I came to Greenville on the bus and got bargain permanent waves. We went to Saluda and Tryon, where I saw some cute cabins; I would like to honeymoon there... I like your new suit... Time flies when I'm with you, and drags when I'm not...

Aug 9, 1940
Daisy in Greenville

I went to a Dinner Party and met a sweet girl who likes you a lot... I enjoyed your Special Delivery letters. Darling, I think you are an old meanie not to want me to enjoy myself without you. But, it's true, I can't. I want you to behave yourself. I'm scared you won't like living in the Village. Wish I were living there with you, but I'd want a ring on my finger of my left hand...

Aug 14, 1940
Daisy in Chester

I'm so glad you like your work and your place. Do the new boys like New York? I miss you so much that it's awful. I gave Isabel a good pep talk about going to Winthrop when she hates it so much. She went home & gave them the works & they're letting her go to business school! She might go in Columbia because Margaret's husband has just joined the Army & they'll be there. He has a good deal of money & they built a new house before they got married... John & Mary are in New York. They are going to see "Hell's A-popping." I'm going to take a business course in Greenville this winter. After I start working, I can do what I please & live by myself. It must be grand not to ask somebody for every cent one spends...

Aug 20, 1940
Daisy in Chester

Hey My Dearest Darling,

I love you. Gosh, it's hot as hell today. I've just had an ice-cold bath & I'm still hot. P. wanted me to go to church with him—I told him to find someone else... You sounded drunk in your last letter; are you broke because of gambling? Wilkie's speech was grand; I wish I could vote for him... I miss you terribly much. I wouldn't work in New York if they'd give me the whole dam place. When I start working, it will be in Greenville. Bob, I think you should play the field. Listen Darling, you might just as well have your fun because it's going to be a hell of a long time before we can even think about getting married... Last night, Hoover, Nell, Pete and I went to Charlotte to the Open-Air Picture Show. It's grand, you just sit on the car and watch, and every car has a sound box. We had a lot of fun. P. has been dating a very young girl... Pete Wy. has been fired because of his marriage...

Aug 21, 1940
Daisy in Chester

You are good to write me so much... My new Dorothy Gray lipstick is "Daredevil." [*Sends an imprint of a kiss.*]

Aug 23, 1940
Daisy in Chester

I am keeping house while Mother's knee is hurting... Do you think they'll call you for the Army? Things keep coming along to add more years before we can really begin to live...

Aug 28, 1940
Daisy in Chester

Kirk left a darling little bird-dog puppy for me to take care of until he comes back. He's like a little baby. His stomach is so fat he can't scratch himself... I'm thrilled that I can come to see you in Washington. I hope it suits Eleanor...

Sept 7, 1940
Bob in NYC

I am kinda peeved at you. I had hoped to hear from you this morning. I wish it were last weekend, and I was with you again. I don't have a dam thing to do tonight. I will never be happy until I am with you for always. Each day I live through just brings that out clearer to me. I played tennis this morning. . . I was thinking about going out, but after seeing you only last weekend, I could not stand anyone else. I may get a date out of sheer desperation. There's nothing else to do, and I can't just sit. You suit me so completely that I'll never be happy without you. . .

All my love for always, Bob

Sept 7, 1940
Daisy in Chester

Hey My Dearest Dear Darling,

The weekend was heaven! Especially when you woke me up Monday morning. When I got on the train, tears were rolling down my face. I'm glad you didn't see me cry. I tried so hard not to, when I was with you. After I got on, a nice-looking man asked me if he could sit with me. I wondered why he didn't sit in one of the vacant seats. We had a big time. He works for the American Tobacco Co., so he had oodles of Luckys and he wanted to give me some, but I wouldn't let him. He got off in Virginia, and bought me a cup of coffee and a ham sandwich. I didn't want him to pay for anything but he insisted, so we ate the whole way to Reidsville, NC, where he got off. He was coming from NY; we talked and laughed the whole way. He said the same things you did about the girls in the North. He said I had a baby face. I didn't like that. He's 30. Bob, I've been thinking a lot about what you said are little things I do that annoy you. I'm scared to marry you because I couldn't stand it if you started hating me... Darling, thanks for taking me around in Washington. I enjoyed every minute of it. I'm sorry you spent so much money on me... Isabel Wy. is pregnant and I envy her...

I love you.

Sept 10, 1940
Bob in NYC

Hey My Dearest Darling,

Something has been on my mind lately. Do you remember when I said in a letter that I found out a lot of little things about you. Did you understand that those things were little acts of yours that I love? I have been under the impression that you are thinking I meant things that irritated me. Last weekend I said something about your kissing me. Darling, I don't mind in the least. I find myself all the time wishing I could see you, the way you move your hands and the way you look at me. Darling, it is not to be expected that we could live together without any friction. We are only human. I know when we do get our chance, we will be completely happy. I would give anything to be able to be with you from day to day. I am really going through hell up here away from you. Sometimes I get frightened about all the time I am wasting by not being with you every day. Tonight, there is a fear in my heart that something is going to happen to keep me from being near you. Usually I can fight off that feeling... I am so put out with Ciba Co. for not sending me to Charlotte, but my hands are tied. Darling, I enjoyed both your letters yesterday. I never have been so glad to hear from you in my life. I sat around Sunday waiting for your Special. Then after I got it, I felt so good and I went to the show. When I returned, I got the other one, and it was swell. It is after twelve, but I don't want to go to bed. I am having more fun writing to you. Your letters would be wonderful if they just said, "I love you". I will never grow tired of hearing you say that. Please don't ever stop... I played bridge tonight and talked about war. Maybe that's what got me scared. I wish you were here to comfort me—childish, and I wouldn't admit it to anyone but you. When I'm with you, nothing scares or worries me... You're the woman I want behind me... I like the news from home. Doesn't it make you feel funny to see everybody else getting married? It hurts my heart that we can't go ahead yet, and one of these days I will kick over the traces... It's awful to think of spending the winter without you...

I want you to be my wife.

In September 1940, the first peacetime military draft in U. S. history was started for young men ages 21-35. Other events included the following: Jews in Germany were required to wear yellow stars for identification, Britain was being bombed, Italian forces launched an invasion of Egypt, and the Japanese occupied French Indochina.

Sept, 1940
Daisy in Greenville

I started Business School, and am crazy about it. I've already completed 7 lessons in Bookkeeping. For the first time in my life, I'm doing something worthwhile. I believe I'll like working and supporting myself. . . I imagine that Ciba doesn't send you to Charlotte because they think you're going to be called into the Army. Don't let it worry you, because you know you're good. It would be wonderful to have you wake me up every morning as you did in Washington, but it's going to be years before that will be possible. . . No, it doesn't make me feel strange to think about people here getting married while we wait. I'm glad they're taking the chance because life is much too short. I admire them. I bought a red feather hat, black shoes and pocket book for $8. 00. We went to see a friend of Harriet's who has 3 children, age 2 and under, and is very happy. She and her husband are lovebirds. For every date out, he sends her flowers. She wants me to meet her brother. 3 babies in 33 months. I want to do as well.

Sept 12, 1940
Bob in NYC

Hey My Dearest Darling,

I enjoyed your letter so much today. How does it feel to be on your way toward being independent? It gives me a lot of satisfaction to know that I am supporting myself. It feels so good to be able to do the things you want to. I didn't mind in the least taking you out in Washington. I had wanted to do that for a long time. I get so much for my money with you. I have spent more than that in one evening, and didn't have near the good time I had with you. I am glad you appreciate it. I've been cooking—a dime's worth of potatoes will last all week. Tonight, I had clam chowder, fried Spam, lettuce and tomatoes, potato salad, coffee, milk and toast. For .25¢, I got all I wanted. . . George is still gone, and I'm lonely by myself. Thank you for news of home. What made Nick change to Roosevelt? I am hoping the whole country will change to him. I can't see anyone but him in the White House. Daisy, please try as hard as you can in your business course. I hope you won't have to work the four or five years you said you would like to, but anything might happen. I want to be sure to have enough to make you happy before I ask you to marry me. I shouldn't talk about that with everything so uncertain, but it is constantly on my mind and just slips out. It seems so funny how everything goes on just the same after you leave home. It seemed like everything would be different when I went away, but life goes on just the same. . . After all, I am just a cog in a machine. I slip out and someone else takes my place. The only thing I am sure of is that I still keep my place with you. You are looking at me with the cutest smile now (from your picture). When I am sure of you, you always smile.

    All my love for always, Bob

Sept 12, 1940
Daisy Hampton, Chester, to Daisy,
Greenville

Hope you like your course. I'm sorry I mailed Bob's letter late... My knee hurts... I washed your clothes. I visited B. L., and drank a Coca-Cola. The house needs a good cleaning... Write a list of what you want me to send. Dad sends love.

Love, Mother

Sept 14, 1940
Bob in NYC

Hey my Dearest Darling,

I hate weekends without you. The moon is so pretty tonight. It makes me lonesome for you. I am going downtown in the morning to take my physical examination. As soon as I get my report filled, I am going to send it off and volunteer for service. I can't hold off any longer. I have reason to believe that as soon as the draft bill is passed, I will be called... This is just between you and I for the present... I don't want to put out any reports until I am certain when I am going. I don't want to get anyone stirred up until everything is set. I just had to let you know. You are such a part of me that I always think of you first when I have to decide anything. I don't know how this is going to affect you and I, but it certainly can't be any worse. I hate to interrupt your work, but I will have to see you before I go. I thought about taking a week off, but I will need that extra money to get started. It is going to be kinda tough sledding for a while at least. Darling, I feel certain that I am doing the right thing. There has been a lot of doubt before in my mind, but everything is clear now. The prospect of looking forward to this step hasn't been pleasant and I am kinda glad it is here at last. I have Mr. Parker's word that he will do his best to give me my job back whenever I want. Well, Darling, wish me luck. Maybe I will be stationed close to home. I love you with all my heart.

Sept 17, 1940
Bob in NYC

Hey My Dearest Darling,

I enjoyed your letter, and hope your work won't interfere with writing me. I sure am glad you like your studies. It is a lot of fun to be really doing something, isn't it? You will have fun on your first job. I heard a woman of thirty-five tell of her first job. She had to hold an old man's hand all day. . . I am patiently waiting until I am called. The sooner, the better. Tell Nick that I have finally volunteered. I know he will like it. I guess you are right; Parker couldn't send me to Charlotte when there is every possibility of my going into the Army. Did I get too sentimental in my letter last night? I couldn't hold back my feelings. . . It looks like that 1942 marriage of ours won't have much of a chance. Still you never can tell, something may give us a break or maybe I can get a little spunk! My face is sun burnt, but it's better than sitting around here, or in some show. I feel swell tonight. I'm in good shape and back to my usual weight. . . I want to hear news of your friends. . . Keep on loving me.

Sept 17, 1940
Daisy in Greenville

Last night I had an awful nightmare about you. it was much too real. I dreamed you died. It was such a long dream. I dreamed I tried to get your home on the phone & the line was busy, so I called R. C. When I woke up, I was drenched in a cold clammy sweat and tears were all over my face. Even my hair was wet. I was so relieved to wake up and find it wasn't true... I'm glad you're going into the Army before they draft you. I hoped you would. Darling, I'm real proud of you and know you passed your physical exam...

Sept 18, 1940,
Bob in NYC

Hey My Dearest Darling

I want to see you, be with you, and talk every day. I love to tell you my troubles and ideas... I cooked a swell dinner- would you like to marry a good cook? The papers are really full of this draft business... I am expecting to see the Reserve officers called out any day now... It's strange, living when there is a war going on; I worry about the future, and where all this will lead. One thing I am sure of, and that is, for some years to come, we are going to live under a tension or strain, and the old type of living our natural lives seems to be gone forever... I can't see how the world is going to get over this war and be the same as it was before. I hope you don't mind my rambling; I love to tell you my thoughts. I have decided that when I come back to my job, I am going to hold out for Charlotte or nothing. I think I will have a right to ask that much. I couldn't possibly come back to the life I am leading right now. If I have to stay up here this fall and winter, I will grow to hate it. There's not enough happiness for me here. I can't find the right kind of people to run around with. If we were married, I could enjoy every day... My philosophy on life is tangled up tonight. I hope I'm not boring you. I want to tell our children some day about all this, how Daddy lived in New York for a time, and then went in the Army. I want to grow old with you, but I can't see the way clearly, and it worries me. I will keep hoping and doing my best to make it all come true. I'm set on having a decent life for you before I ask you to be my wife. I wouldn't want you to do without anything. Getting success is taking a long, tough time...

Sept, 1940 date unknown

I'm lost without you. I dream of you every time I go to sleep... I am discouraged, and can't work it out to be near you... Sometimes I feel as if I should not have come to NY. I love you more than ever...

Sept 20, 1940
Daisy Hampton in Chester

I have pain in my legs and the doctor told me to wear elastic stockings. I bought a hat... Take care of yourself... We are having a drought...

["Ultimatum letter"]

Date unknown
Bob in NYC

Hey My Dearest Darling,

I have just finished reading your letter and frankly I am worried. Daisy, I have been letting things drift along until I could kinda see my way clear about this Army business. . . But I think it is about time I took a hand in things. I have been watching a change take place in our relationship. I don't know whether you have noticed it or not, but since the first of last summer you have given me plenty of chances to break off our love affair. Darling, if you feel way down in your heart that you would rather not go on, if it is too much of a burden for you to go on loving me under such difficult circumstances, then for goodness sakes, tell me so. Then, and only then, will I stop writing you and try to stop loving you. If I didn't love you so dam much, I would have ended it long before this. If I didn't feel that you think of me rightfully as your future husband, I wouldn't even answer your last letter. Darling, listen to me now seriously, I believe that you think I am the one man in this world for you. Okay then, I am going to do everything I can to make a place for you at my side. I can't say that I want to marry next year. But I will say that by this time next year I will be certain of my position, and be able to offer you something definite. Darling, I wish you wouldn't make me show my hand. It would be much better if you would trust me, and not worry about when we can get married. Now Daisy, cut out all the foolishness about waiting five or six years before we get married. You know darn well that after I have been out of school—2 ½ or 3 years, I will be able to support you. What kind of man do you think I am that I have to wait five or six years until I can have the girl I love, at my side? I know the fact that everyone around home is getting married has something to do with your feelings. That is why I asked you how you felt about it not so long ago. I could have stayed around home, married you, and lived an ordinary life, but I want something better than that, for our children and us. Now Daisy, here's the situation in a nutshell. If your love for me has died, we will call it quits, otherwise, Darling, you are to get such thoughts as were in your last letter completely out of your mind. We are not going to wait four or five years. I really and truly love you and want you to be my wife, when the right time comes, and I believe it is coming soon. If you are not willing to wait two or three years on me, then maybe we had better stop now. Darling, I am mad at you tonight but I still love you dearly. Another boy was sent to Charlotte today... I am going out and get tight tonight. I should be at the boy's apartment now, but I had to write you first. Don't you think that is nice of me? I am trying to be as forceful as I can. I wish I had you here with me. I would probably want to spank you. You have no right to send me a letter like the one you sent today. Don't do it again unless you want to call it quits. I can't get you to realize that I no longer think of you as a girl to go out with, and see when I go home. To me, Darling, you are the one woman I want as my wife and the one woman I want to spend the rest of my life bringing happiness. Darling, this letter is more or less as an ultimatum... Come back to me completely and trust me or don't come back at all. I don't want you and I to drift apart. We both would feel like hell if I wanted to marry you and you had married someone else. Daisy, all this is putting seeds of doubt in my mind about your love for me, so write soon and let me know that you love me just as strong as ever.

As always, I love you. Bob

["Answer to Ultimatum"]

> Sept 22, 1940
> Daisy in Greenville

Dear Sir:

I got your letter of Ultimatum this morning... I'll try not to ever mention marriage to you again. I'm sorry... I'll cease having my own ideas, and always agree with you... We'll just be two people in love with no thought for the future. We'll go back to how we were when you were at Clemson. Lots of Love, Daisy

> Sept 23, 1940
> Bob in NYC

[Torn up bits of a letter, saved in the envelope]

> Sept 25, 1940
> Daisy in Columbia

Hey My Dearest Darling,

Bob, I refuse to stop writing you until you tell me you don't love me, and I hope that will never be. Darling, I don't know what was the matter with me; I'm sorry. Will you forgive me? It seems as if you're always forgiving me for something I've done... Just keep on loving me. If we stopped writing and drifted apart, we might never find each other again. I couldn't let that happen when it's all my fault that we're beginning to drift right now. When I feel like this, I want to go home where life is simple; where Mother & Daddy have each other, and always will.

Sept 26, 1940
Daisy in Columbia

I'm not going to school today because I feel terrible after reading your letter. Bob, may I come back to you completely? If you want me to, I'll even get down on my knees the next time I see you, and ask you to keep on loving me. Darling, when I think about losing you, it doesn't matter if we have to wait 20 years to get married. Darling, I'm beginning to understand how my letter must have hurt you. I say, from the bottom of my heart, I'm so sorry... I tore up your letter because if I kept it, I would read it a million times and know every time it was my fault. I want you back... Keep my picture... Tear up the awful letters I wrote...

Date unknown
Bob in NYC

Hey My Dearest Darling,

I have just received your Special and my heart is right again. For the first time in a week, I am able to breathe freely. I have been scared to death since I wrote you, and I am so glad that you still want me. A load has lifted from my mind. I am going to forget that we ever wrote to each other like we did. Sweetheart, I wish I could take you in my arms tonight and show you how much I care. Your letter was the most marvelous I have ever received from you. I could jump up and shout with joy right this minute. I am so happy. You won't have to come back, Darling, for you are with me and always will be. One night I cried myself to sleep, and the other nights I almost never went to sleep. I dam near lost all my ambition, self-confidence and everything. But, now I am strong again. I will write you a nice long letter tomorrow, and tell you how much better the world looks after hearing from you... Our love is still safe and strong... Good night, my dearest.

Yours only, Bob

Sept 27, 1940
Daisy in Greenville

It's been terribly cold. I've finished 19 lessons in my workbook and started on my Practice set [in business school]. I like it. Went to see "Brigham Young" this afternoon. It was good but it wore me out. They rode way out to Utah in covered wagons. The hardships they went through were terrible. I dated a Clemson grad last night—real tall and nice looking. He said he was offered a job in New York, and wouldn't take it for anything. Darling, I still haven't heard from you and I'm going to keep on writing until you tell me you'd rather I wouldn't. Then I'll stop for all time. When you tell me we're finished, I'll send your picture and pin back, and burn all your letters. That sounds awful to me, but if you think we had better end it, I want it to be for good... No one else can ever take my love for you away; it's part of me. If you want to end it, that's final, because there will never be any going back, it would never be the same, there would always be something lacking, and I don't want even the smallest thing lacking in my marriage. I've cried a good deal since I got your letter yesterday but tonight, I'm a little bit past tears. I'm not expecting much of a reply, if any, from you, because I realize you've said just about all you're going to say but I'm still hoping. I'm going to Chester for the weekend. We'll take Mother to the doctor in Charlotte for her leg. My place really is at home helping them because they're getting old and neither one is very well. I hope you pass your Army tests with flying colors. Darling, if you have decided we're finished, I'd rather you didn't see me when you come through on your way to the Army. Everyone else is in bed; I'm sitting by the fireplace. The ticking of the old clock seems to be saying, "I love him" over and over. . . I'm sorry they sent someone else to Charlotte. I understand that you may want to be "fancy free"; I felt like that when I was 15.

All My Love for always, Me

Not dated
Bob to Daisy

I hope you know by now that everything is forgiven; I love you with all my heart. . . I enjoyed today, saying to myself that everything is okay. . . George is back. We went to see "Freaky Partners." I miss going out with you at home, and I want a life with you. . .

Sept 30, 1940
Bob in NYC

Hey My Dearest Darling,

It has been thrilling to get those three Specials from you. Yesterday, I spent the afternoon at the Fair and got your letter when I came in. . . I had a quiet day today, looking around and taking life easy. It is the first time in ages I have spent a day just loafing. Usually I have to go to a show or something to break the monotony. Maybe after a hectic week, I know that our love still holds and keeps on growing. It means so much, to know that I can keep working and planning for that day when you will be mine. I became interested in art this past weekend—paintings and the like. Isn't that funny, can you imagine me wandering through an art gallery looking at old paintings? It is kinda silly. Me, who has only been interested in loving you, enjoying myself at dances, and working. But there I was. Saturday, I spent four hours in the Masterpieces of Art exhibit at the Fair, and this afternoon I stayed in the Metropolitan Museum of Art for two and a half hours. I have learned what types I like. One is the old clear-cut masterpieces of the Italians, and the other is the natural paintings of everyday American life. . . This is hardly more than a passing fancy, so don't get worried. I still don't like living up here. I would like it if you were with me. My heart breaks when I see a couple enjoying themselves. . . I am slipping as a dancer, and want to dance with you lots. . . I saw the castle and the view in Central Park by the museum; someday I will show it all to you. I feel wonderful knowing I will never lose you. I love you my Darling completely.

All my love for always, Bob

Bob in NYC

Oct 3, 1940
Bob in NYC

Hey My Dearest Darling,

I hope everything is all right. I haven't heard from you since Saturday. In your last letter, you still hadn't heard from me so I don't know what the situation is. But Darling, when I realized how much I must have hurt you by writing like I did, I swore to myself that never again would I let the fear of losing you worry me and make me almost go crazy. I know you love me, so I am going to keep out of my mind all the worries I can. It is hard to do when you don't write, or when you write strange letters, but Darling I am going to try my best. In other words, I trust you completely. Everything is still the same up this way. That makes it hard, but I am getting used to making myself take things like this. I haven't heard from the Army and still don't know whether I am coming or going. The only thing I can do is to say it will all turn out for the best.

Do you think that I have failed or not done my best in making my decisions these past four months? God knows I have tried to do what's right, but I never seem to get anywhere. I would have gone in the Army back in June if I hadn't let common sense make me stick to my job. I am going to write tonight and see if I can't get some action from the Army. If it is coming, then I wish it would come on. Patience is one of the things that I don't own. . . . I miss you; it's been raining and cold. . . .

Things at the lab are slowing down. . . . I hope your mother is better. I've heard from Alice that everyone is married but Hoover, Pete, Buck and Rube. . . . It's harder to make money than last year. I'll be able to save when I have you to hold me down. . . .

Write a lot and I will too. All my love for always, Bob

Oct 4, 1940
Daisy in Greenville

I enjoyed your letter yesterday so much. Yes, Darling, I can imagine you looking at pictures. You ought to know something about good pictures because your mother painted such lovely ones. I like to go to art exhibits. I went in Columbia whenever I got a chance. I'd like to have gone with you in New York. . . You said you were scared last week that you had lost me. How do you think I felt about what I said to you? I never realized that something I said could hurt me so bad afterwards. I knew I'd lost you for all times because if you stopped writing to me, it would be over for good. I'm so glad you forgave me and took me back into your heart. I love you. The Cotton Festival is going on here. We took Patti and little Kirkwood to see the Parade this afternoon. . . A crowd of men from Kirk's New York firm gave a big banquet at the Poinsett last night. They had an open bar and all the trimmings. Kirk made a speech. . . Have you heard from the Army? I could almost see you marching when the N. G. marched today. I love you more than ever, and what happened knocked me to my senses. . .

Oct 8, 1940
Bob in NYC

I want to be with you and kiss you. I have a powerful love for you and you have a hold on me. . . I saw "Dubarry was a Lady" yesterday, and wanted you there. I walked along Times Square and saw a friend from home who is in the Army. He is stationed on Long Island. We had dinner together and talked about the Army. I feel better and can see my way clear. . . Darling, I really and truly am glad that you wouldn't let us break up. I feel better about everything than I have in years.

All my love for always, Bob

Oct 9, 1940
Daisy in Greenville

Hey My Dearest Darling,

Wish you were here. I'm tired as hell! I did 13 reports and a trial balance today. I have 6 more to do and I'll be through with my first Practice set. When I do 19 reports in my book and another practice set, I'll be through bookkeeping & ready for shorthand. I'm doing well. Darling, I enjoyed your letter. You didn't hurt me; I deserved everything you said & a lot more. I was so scared you were gone for good, that I didn't have time to be hurt. I tore it up anyway. I don't think you've made wrong decisions this past year because you do what you think is best. If it turns out to be good, you're ahead, and if it turns out the other way, you've learned what to do next time. Darling, I think you're doing fine. . . I know it's hard to save in a big city with so many things to do, and you should have a good time because you're young and there isn't someone depending on you. . .

Date unknown
Bob in NYC

Things are still dragging on for me, but I hope this will change after the election. I hope I am not still here by Christmas. I don't enjoy life in this city without you. . . I saw President Roosevelt at Madison Square Garden. . . I argue with folks at the lab; I want him to win. I'm glad to hear that you are working hard in the Business Course. . . I'm eating a lot; I have gained to 165. . . I'm not writing to anybody but you. We have been apart for 16 months. That is a long time, when I used to see you every two or three weeks. I have learned what it is to want someone until it hurts deep down inside. You are the one person I want to live with for the rest of my life. . .

Oct. 10, 1940
Daisy in Greenville

Hey My Dearest Darling,

I know how you feel, wanting to be with the one you love. Wonderful when you're with them, but terrible when you're alone, which is most of the time. . . I am living from one day to the next with the main object of getting a job when I finish my business course. I haven't even thought about our future since I told you I couldn't anymore. Isn't that good? I used to think about it all the time, but now it's become a blank. I think I'm doing well. I hope to have an apt. with some other girls when I start working. . .

Patti and Kirkwood are growing and so cute: I would like to have a little boy. Kirk & Harriet are so much in love; Harriet wishes they'd married sooner...

I'd like to live my life over and do so many things I didn't, and not do a lot of the things I did. Wouldn't you? I wonder if I've learned anything in my 18 years. I'm beginning to realize that when you can't have something you want more than anything in the world, you make something else to take its place...

Oct 11, 1940
Daisy Hampton, Chester, to Daisy, Greenville

Dr. Malone died Tues. evening & was buried yesterday from the house... I am going to the hospital for a friend in Charlotte. Not sure what I will wear. I made pickles to-day...

Love from us all to all, Mother

Not dated
Bob to Daisy

I am going to vote for the first time this year. I made 100 on the literacy test...

Oct 12, 1940
Daisy in Greenville

I enjoyed your airmail to-day... I'm having fun—went out to a nightclub with someone who roomed near you at Clemson...

Oct 14, 1940
Bob in NYC

Hey My Dearest Darling,

I was playing bridge when your letter came. Darling, I am so glad you are having a good time. It makes me feel like hell, knowing that somebody else is taking you out when I would like so much to be the one. I hope those guys realize how lucky they are.

My foot is just about well. I am relieved too, for I had feared it would keep me out of the Army. The salve I got from the Doctor seems to have done the trick. I miss you, and go out to pass the time. I went on a party in the Village, got drunk and came home at five, but it wasn't much fun. Would rather be with you... I went to the Dodgers game, saw George Raft and Sonja Heine... I had a letter from the Army, which said to sit tight and not bother them anymore; my application has been received... Tonight, I had country sausage, grits, tomatoes, fried sweet potatoes, diced beets, milk and coffee. I feel out of it, and would rather be back in South Carolina where everybody talks my language...

Oct 14, 1940
Nick to Daisy, Greenville

Dear Sis',

Find enclosed ck for 72.00 divided as follows; School 50.00 Expenses 10.00 Your mother 12.00

Tell Kirk to come over Sat & get some arrangements made for feeding his cattle. Your mother says this is all she can send you this month, so be careful of it. Hope you are OK & doing all right. Suppose you will be home last of week. Love to all. JNS

Oct. 15, 1940
Bob in NYC

Hello, I love you. . . I have been jitterbugging by myself tonight. I would like to dance more often, but there's no inexpensive place to go. I am still sitting around waiting for the Army to call. I have been waiting for almost a month, ready to go, and it is really nerve-wracking. I think that I will get to see you before I go, and the prospect of seeing you almost any weekend, makes the waiting worse. . . Gosh, I've thought about everything I have done in the past several years.

My thoughts returned a million times to when we have been together. I wanted you so bad that I could almost feel you here beside me. What I really need is to have a weekend with you. I am getting so I can't be satisfied with a thing I do. The moon was beautiful tonight. I took a walk in the park, and thought of you. . . I have always heard that your happiest days are in college or high school. Still, I believe I am going to find happier days, and they will be with you. Darling, I hope you don't mind my rambling on like this. There is nothing to write about unless I tell you my thoughts. . . I will get to see you at least by Thanksgiving. . . I love you Darling, more than enough.

Oct 18, 1940
Daisy in Greenville

I had fun last weekend going out with Sissy & Shine, and dating your classmate from Clemson. We danced 'til 3. I went with him to dinner at Clemson on Sunday and met a lot of people. Darling, I wish you would cuss me out about drinking so much Sat. night. I drank perfectly straight up without anything... I'm glad we didn't bust up because it doesn't make any difference to me now how long we have to wait. My interests are changing a lot. I haven't been with you but off & on for the last year and I'm learning to have a good time with other people and not get bored stiff at everything they say.

Darling, what I've just said doesn't mean I don't love you as much as ever. 'Cause I do & always will.

All My Love Always, Me

Oct. 18, 1940
Bob in NYC

Hey My Dearest Darling,

I've been showing the town to my sister's roommate for the past two nights—out until four o'clock the first night and two the next. The Rainbow Room is breathtaking; I wished you were there. It was my first trip to a big nightspot and a swell experience. I have come to the conclusion that I am not much of a person to go out with. I am so much in love with you that I never stop thinking of you when I am out with someone else.

I would like to show you New York... Can you imagine paying ten or twelve dollars, at least, for dinner and a few drinks? It is just too steep for me...

I love you Sweet, Lots & Lots, Loads & Loads and bushels!

Oct 19, 1940

It was wonderful hearing your voice again. I was walking on air for the rest of the night. When I started talking to you, I forgot everything I had planned to say... I feel relaxed for the first time in weeks.

I trust you and wouldn't tell you what to do. I know some of the men you're going out with... Be careful and don't forget that I love you, or let the good times interfere with your business course. I won't cuss you out for drinking when I do the same thing... I have a date tonight with a little gal from downstairs...

Oct 21, 1940
Daisy in Greenville

Your call meant so much to me. Oh, Darling, I didn't want to go out with Louis after I heard your voice. I want to be with you so bad. I try to enjoy being with other people, but I can't. It's impossible, loving you the way I do. I'm glad you called me, but I hate to think of the money you spent. I wanted to say, "I love you" so bad, but Harriet's aunt & uncle were sitting right here listening to every word. After you called, Louis & I went to a football game, & rode out to the airport to watch the big transports come in. It wasn't any fun. All the time I was thinking about you, and how good your voice sounded... I love you. You haven't kissed me in so long. It seems years...

Oct 23, 1940
Daisy in Greenville

Hey My Dearest Darling,

I want to be with you, and never let you go... I enjoyed your letter so much yesterday, but I wish you had blessed me out, because it is a great deal of difference between your taking a drink and my taking one. Even though I don't, except about every 5 months. Darling, you know I'm careful. Why, I've got too much pride to do something I couldn't tell you about, and besides, Darling, I'm in love with you and don't want anyone else to touch me. Don't you know that by now?

I saw "Foreign Correspondent" last night. I expect to hear any day that you're in the Army...

Oct 23, 1940
Bob in NYC

Hey My Dearest Darling,

I wish I could call you every night—it's money well spent, and more fun for me than going out. You make my heart jump with joy when you tell me you want no one but me. I thought I would have been in the Army by now. I'm mad that I can't plan anything; I would like to take you to the Clemson-Furman football game... I've had a cold due to the weather... I'm hoping to get orders for down South soon...

I've waited too long to get my topcoat cleaned; I really need a wife, and that's in my mind all the time. I can't get over the thrill of hearing your voice over the telephone. Gosh, you don't realize how wonderful a telephone is until you feel as if you are right beside someone who is miles away...

Oct 26, 1940
Daisy in Greenville

I saw 'Knute Rockney" at the late show last night with Louis. It was grand. We went for a long ride and I didn't get in until after one. I went to the show this afternoon with his sister and he brought me home... I missed you last night, had trouble sleeping, and felt bad. You're the only man I'll ever want...

Oct 27, 1940
Bob in NYC

I went on a stag party last night—six of us bowled, and then played cards until four in the morning. I didn't drink much. I missed you when I was walking home in the moonlight...

Oct 28, 1940

My Sunday is complete when I get your letter... I had a date in Jersey and went to the Fair today. It was such a large crowd—I had to help a girl near me who fainted...

Oct 29, 1940
Daisy in Greenville

Nick & Daisy were very disappointed to hear you haven't been sent to Guam or Alaska... I enjoy airmail but don't waste money because I don't get it any sooner... I got a blue satin blouse and a red sweater...

Oct 31, 1940

[*A small, formal invitation to Bob for a woman's party at a hotel on Broadway.*]

Nov 1, 1940
Daisy in Greenville

Darling, I miss you so dam much, it's awful. It has been a long time, hasn't it? Sometimes I wonder how everything is going to work out... All we can do is hope for the best & let things drift along for several more years as they've done in the past. Darling, I've gotten pretty good—I never think of being married to you, it's always just going with you and writing. Before I met you, I had a horror of going with someone for ages, but never getting anywhere. It's not really as bad as I imagined. Sometimes I wonder why you aren't tired of me; I guess it's because we see so little of each other and at such long intervals. This is our third year, isn't it? I had better hush before I say a lot of things I'll regret in the morning. I'm in a "what's the use" mood. Ever have one? Don't, it's not much fun. It started by thinking about when I was in High School. What a different person I was then. I wish I was like that now. I saw everything through "rose colored glasses."

I'm sorry I made such a mess of this letter. I'll try to write a better one next time.

All My Love, Me

Nov 1, 1940
Bob in NYC

Hey My Dearest Darling,

Your letter today was just what I needed to cheer me up. This election is getting on my nerves. Several of us have been wearing Roosevelt buttons and it has really created a stir. Maybe we are sticking our necks out, but I can't stand to see those guys flaunting their Wilkie buttons all the time. We really have some hot arguments. I can't argue with them anymore. I am just going to sit tight until elections, and then whoever is elected will be my president. Oh, Darling, I need you so bad tonight. I have the darndest desire that I know only you can fulfill. Sometimes I get so mad with myself for being way up here where I can't even get to see you, that I want to give up and go back to you. Darling, maybe I am a little blue tonight. I will be all right in the morning...

Nov 2, 1940
Daisy in Greenville

When I last wrote, I felt blue, like the color of this stationery. I'm sorry you haven't had the news you want, but your luck is about to change...

I made a Halloween supper for Patti and little Kirk. Kirk took us downtown, and the streets were full of children dressed up. I hope we can marry before we're too old to have children. When we're married, let's always celebrate everything. . .

Date unknown,
1940 Bob in NYC

I am not a bit better off than I was last night, so look out for another blue letter. It is either that or no letter at all. Daisy, you are the only one I can really open my heart to. Gosh, Darling, I wish I could do this in person; it would be so much more comforting. I really need you to cheer me up. . . You know I don't think I am anything extra special either in my work, or my military, but I am better than average and I can't understand why I am still sitting here. . . I have had so dam many disappointments these last few months, that tonight I am almost at the end of my rope. If I don't get my orders in another week, I don't know what I will do. A friend sent in his application after I did, and has already gotten his orders. My time is coming, but I can't stand waiting much longer. This kind of stuff makes a fellow want to get drunk. If I only knew that I was worth a dam, and that everything would break for me, I wouldn't give a dam how much longer I have to wait. I don't even know what the folks down at the lab think of me. Darling, do you see the position I am in? I can't think of marrying you until I am sure I am on my way up. I couldn't bear to have you tied to a failure. I wouldn't talk to anyone else like this. I know you will understand my feelings. I am not doing this to get sympathy; just to get it off my chest, and you are the only one I can turn to. I feel better just knowing you will read this. My desire for you is strong tonight. I am so dam mixed up about this Army business, and I'm worried about when I will get my chance to be with you for always. It makes the ache in my heart for you that much worse. . . If I could just spend this night in your arms, I could face the world tomorrow much better. Don't worry too much about me. I'm down tonight but I'll be back up tomorrow and I know everything will be alright but I don't know when. . .

Date unknown
Daisy in Greenville

Please don't ever use that awful word in connection with yourself, because Darling you're not a failure, and never will be. You've only been working a little over a year and who do you know that has worked just that long and gotten all the breaks? No one does. Listen, Darling, do your work at the lab the best you can and don't give a dam what the folks there think of you. That doesn't matter just so long you think you're good. You've got to realize that there are going to be plenty more disappointments in life that will make those seem terribly small, but there will be plenty of good breaks to make up for them. Darling, how much fun do you think life would be if everything we wanted was handed to us? It would be pretty dull. Ellen C. goes with a boy who went to Clemson; he's waiting to be called and expects it will be months. Please don't get drunk every time something goes wrong. Bob, that scares me.

[Bob is now in the Army]

Date unknown
Bob at Ft. Benning, Ga.

I sure would like to be with you this weekend. We have a holiday tomorrow... Darling, I regret so much that I can't be with you more often. God knows I want to. Everything is going to be better than it was last year but I still won't get much time off. We are entitled to two and one-half days leave per month. I will be in Greenville on Thanksgiving—and am going to write for tickets to the game. Maybe I will get to stay the weekend. The day with you last week went so dam fast. I feel as if I just dropped in and said hello. Anyway, for either Thanksgiving or Christmas I will have three whole days to spend with you. Won't that be swell! I am staying with a bunch of officers in an old frame building that may fall down any minute. We're hoping it keeps the wind out. I am not staying in a tent, thank Goodness. I haven't done a dam thing so far, except get my uniforms and go through an inspection, but next week I will really get to work...

Not dated
Bob in Ga.

I can almost see my way clear to happiness with you. I am on the way to being a good officer. I'm glad we're only three hundred miles apart... I feel funny having a bunch of men call me sir and do the things I tell them. I am learning to handle men, and give instructions... We won't have to wait long to get married. Harry and Melba came down to look for housing. I saw a girl I knew from last summer; I hope to have a date next weekend...

Nov 12, 1940
Daisy in Greenville

Shine is at Fort Benning. He told Sissy he would be coming to see her soon, so maybe you could come too. I enjoyed seeing you on Wednesday so much... Isabel has invited me to some good parties in Charlotte. I'm not telling anyone how I feel but you, because I know we won't get married for four years and too much can happen between now and then. It's foolish to talk about something that may never happen. For one thing, you'll be in the Army more than any year by the looks of things. I'm in a rotten mood...

Remember you told me to make you save some money? Bob, you're old enough to know what you want to do, without me trying to tell you. It's your money and you should do what you want to with it. If you want to throw it all away, well, I have no right to tell you what to do, and you might resent it. I'm only the girl that loves you with all my heart. I understand that you're very busy, so I won't expect many letters. I'm going out with Louis tonight. He's really nice, but I can't see why he wants to take me out. I do feel good when I walk beside him because he's so tall... I love you.

Not dated
Bob at Ft Benning

Shine and I will probably come up for a weekend... We enjoyed a dance at the Officers' Club. Darling, are you still a little mad at me? I hope not. If there's anything about me that irritates you, will you tell me? I would like to try to improve. I want you to love me stronger than ever. I will start training troops tomorrow... I saw "Andy Hardy Meets Debutante."

Date unknown
Bob at Ft. Benning

I have been trying to tell you that things are shaping up for us much better than I ever expected. Darling, do you realize that I am now in a position to really plan toward our marriage? I have those breaks I've been talking about, and things are going to pick up now. I want to marry you about this time next year. By then I will be all set. I am going to pay Eleanor the $90 that I owe her by February, and from then on, I will save just for us. We can't get married right away because I will need a car if I stay in the Army for more than a year. Everything is so high, and quarters are so hard to find, that it would be almost impossible for me to bring you here. Also, I want to have a little money saved up to start our married life. So, Darling, there is nothing keeping us apart that I can't fix in this first year. I am laying all my cards on the table, because I can't have you thinking that it will be three or four years before we get married. Your letter hurt like hell. Please don't think like that again. Just say to yourself that in one more year, you and I will be together for always. I am so happy down here mainly because I see my way clear, and it is like a heavy load has lifted off my heart. I haven't been out drinking since I left New York, except with you, and I really don't expect to, except once in awhile. Everything I do is to make it better for us. I don't want you feeling blue; soon everything is going to be swell. Bye Darling.

All my love for always, Bob

In November 1940, the British reinforced their army in the desert in North Africa. The Germans continued to bomb England at night: it was especially destructive in Coventry, Liverpool and Southampton. In the U. S., Franklin D. Roosevelt was elected to a third term.

Nov. 18, 1940
Bob at Ft. Benning

Hey My Dearest Darling,

I enjoyed talking to you this afternoon. I hope you don't think I am a silly fool, but I just had to call you up. Darling, I love you with all my heart. I don't think you realize how much I have settled down. I don't expect to do much running around down here. When the time comes that I am able to ask you to be my wife, I will do it and then you can decide whether I am worth giving up all the plans you will have made. Meanwhile, I will go on giving you all the love I have. I'm not coming up at Thanksgiving—I prefer to take three or four days at Christmas. I had dinner downtown, and played bridge with Bischoff, Harry & Melba Raysor. I introduced Melba to a nice crowd in Columbus so she will have some girlfriends. I wish you could come down some weekend and meet these folks. I have been thinking that it would work out swell. I could get you a place to stay uptown, so you wouldn't have to stay at a hotel. You would like Melba and my captain's wife from Laurens. . . I am so glad to be back down South again. It really makes me feel good to run into people that I know. . . It's been expensive to get outfitted, and I'm glad I got two hundred bucks from Ciba. Otherwise, I would have been in debt before I got started.

Yesterday, I took out my first detail to set off 25 smoke pots for an Infantry School Problem. I didn't have to do much because Major Ford designated where the pots were to be placed. This morning, when we were out in the field, I didn't do anything but run around and try to look intelligent. . . Did you know that you still are in my thoughts constantly? This morning, I found myself wondering what you were doing. I was sitting down beside a fire trying to get warm, when all of a sudden, I found myself wanting to be with you. . . I love you Darling, more than enough

Nov 18, 1940
Daisy in Greenville

Darling, I was thrilled to death when you called me last night. I'm sorry I wrote you such a terrible letter, but I was so dam mad that you thought I was trying to rush you into something. I'm sorry. I was so excited I can hardly remember anything you said. I love you. Only you. You know I'll marry you as soon as you ask me, but lots of times I don't want you to know that I love you that much. I try to keep my emotions under control. I have to, or I'd go crazy. I love you with all my heart. I'll go to Chester and Charlotte for Thanksgiving—I can't have a good time with anyone but you.

I played bridge with some married friends who are about to have babies. I want you to see my new hat, but Dad didn't like it.

Nov 19, 1940

I enjoyed your letter today but I felt so dam mean after I read it—making you, as you say, lay your cards on the table. Darling, I'm sorry. I didn't want you to tell me that until you're ready. Please don't even think of giving me a ring. Things are too expensive even to think about it. I'd much rather have your love than all the rings I've ever seen. I'm sorry you thought I wanted one. I don't even expect one right after we're married. All I want is a wedding ring when the time comes...

Nov. 22, 1940
Bob at FT. Benning

I went to a cocktail party tonight at Colonel Eberle's. I met a bunch of people and had a few good drinks. After that Bishoff, Harry, Melba, and I went to a show. Darling, everything just came up and struck me in the face. All I could think of was why in the hell I didn't have you here with me. I talked to Mrs. Strader, and if you come down, she would put you up. I hope we can arrange it soon... Shine and I are coming to Greenville on the 30th. Does that suit you? Last night I was crazy to see you. Today has been hard for me; no place to go and not getting to see the one I love. It's a waste of time to enjoy myself with anyone but you. I can have a little fun at the dances at the club, but that is because I like to dance and meet people...

Nov 26, 1940
Daisy in Greenville

I am excited about seeing you, and I want to have time alone when you come. I had a double date with Isabel in Charlotte. We went to honky-tonks and drank beer... Dad told me, "Sister, there are two things I want you to forget—that Guy boy and that [Isabel] Darby girl!"

Date unknown
Bob to Daisy

I wish I could be with you tonight. I have something important to say and don't know exactly how to put it on paper. I thought I could wait until I see you next weekend, but I can't. Here goes Darling. Will you marry me? I hate to propose to you so unexpected like, but I can't stand the idea of another year without you. Daisy, what you are getting into will not be easy—We will not have much money, but enough to live on comfortably. We will have to share a small house with Harry Raysor and his wife for a couple of months. We will not have a car, but we will be able to get about, as Harry has a car. Then you will have to live the life of a Second Lt. 's wife. On six days a week, I will get up at six o'clock in the morning and won't be back until six at night, except on Saturday when we have the afternoon off. I am asking a lot for you to give up the plans you have made, but I promise to make you happy. I know we can make a go of it. Next weekend we can make our plans. I am anxious to know how you are going to feel about all of this.

Darling, I hope I am getting this right. It's the most important letter I have ever written in my life. I want you to decide when we are to get married. I want to, at least by the first of the year. I can get four or five days leave at Christmas or New Year's. Daisy, next weekend, you can tell me what your answer is, and we can make our plans... Things have been breaking so fast for us. Less than a month ago, I was wondering when in the hell I could marry you. If you will marry me, I will be the happiest man on this earth... A married Second Lt. receives $183 per month. We can easily live on the $83 each month and have $100 per month outside of living expenses. I know this will be plenty. All that is lacking now is your answer. I love you.

I have been wondering what Nick and Daisy will think... My world will crumble if you don't marry me...

Nov 27, 1940
Daisy in Greenville

Hey My Own Dearest Darling,

You know good and well I'll marry you whenever you say the word, and have no fears about my love for you and our happiness. I intend to do my best to make it last forever. Oh, My Darling, you have no idea how I felt when I read your letter going to town this morning on the bus. Oh, Darling, I'm so dam happy I can't do a thing but think about you. Of course, we can live on $83 a month and we do not need a car. I got along without a car on the farm just fine. I want to pay back Eleanor and not go on a honeymoon or buy an engagement ring. I want to go to Ft. Benning with you, and be alone... I'm willing to share a house with Harry and Melba. I wish it were tonight. I'm ready to marry, and only ask you for a week's notice. I don't want to finish the business course; you're the best boss for a lifetime job. You're not making me give up anything—you'll be giving me great happiness. My answer is yes, and the sooner the better. See, Darling, I don't mean to let you go... What in the world will Nick and Daisy say? Be mad as hell, I guess, but I'm not going to be scared to tell them because I'm proud of our love and I know we'll be happy. Food will cost us $6 a week and we will have plenty for laundry and rent. I'll stop smoking because it is better for me anyway, and we won't go out much. It'll be wonderful and loads of fun...

Dec. 6, 1940

[Telegram from Bob's brother Jimmy and family in Richmond, Va.]

AT NINE TONIGHT WE WILL BREATHE A
PRAYER FOR YOUR AND DAISYS HAPPINESS.

[Daisy & Bob married on Dec 7, 1940. Congratulatory telegrams from sisters and sisters-in-law.]

Dec 27, 1940
R. C. [brother] in Chester to Bob

Well I guess you are enjoying married life. I will join the ranks sometime this spring. I gave Mamie a diamond last week. She was thrilled to death... We are sending you a compote for your wedding and Christmas gift. I hope you all will like it. I also sent you two blankets. Martha Marion and Bill got married Christmas Day. I guess they couldn't wait until summer...

Just RC

III. 1941—Married Life

"When we get married, let's always celebrate everything."

~Daisy, 11/2/1940

✒

Not dated
Eleanor

It was nice to hear from both of you. Keep up the good work and use that stationery. I have credited you with $10. It's grand of both of you to take the stand about your finances. R. C. says he's going to wait to get married until all of us recover from your marriage & Christmas!! He's going to build a house in Lowrys... I'm sending you a set of china...

[Daisy in Chester, to Bob, on Army maneuvers, Ragley, La.]

June 25, 1941

Hey My Dearest Own Darling,

I stood being away from you as long as I could, and got so dam lonesome without you that I called Dad. He said for me to come home, he'd pay my way. I left on the train...

In July 1941, all American men were required to register for the draft. The German army had three million soldiers. Nazi Germany invaded the Soviet Union on June 22, 1941, in the largest German military operation of World War II. Their intent was to destroy the Communist state and the Jews there. SS troops began to kill Jews and Soviet prisoners of war.
"The objective of all training for the period July 1, 1941 to June 30, 1942 is to prepare the Army of the United States for combat under whatever conditions the defense of our country and its possessions may require."
~The US Army GHQ maneuvers of 1941 by Christopher R. Gabel.

> August 6, 1941
> Daisy in Chester

I LOVE U. I still haven't heard any news from you so I guess you're too busy to write. Not hearing from you makes it hard. My life is quiet and nothing much happens. Isabel is 19; she likes one of the soldiers stationed with you. Darling, you really should be here—we listen to the war news as soon as it comes on in the morning and 'til it goes off at night...

> Aug 7, 1941

I want to make love with you, and want you to come back safely... I saw Isabel Wy's twins, and went to church with Alice and Rube...

Virginia [Bob's sister] is going to have a baby... Thank you for the money; my parents have also been giving me some...

> Date unknown
> Bob in Ragley

Hey My Dearest Darling,

I love you Darling, more than ever. I don't feel right not being able to see you every day. I want you so bad tonight. Every time I close my eyes, I can see myself at home with you. It's a good thing that I am busy as hell or else I couldn't stand it without you. Tonight is the first time I have drawn a free breath since we left. As soon as we got in, I had to go to town, buy stuff, gas up, and then go round that night to check up on the boys in the spots. I have so much to talk to you about that I will never put it all in this letter. I want to write you lots, but you will have to be content with a couple short notes whenever I can get them in. We have been going to bed about 10 or 11 and getting up at 4:00 for the last two days, so that, on top of a 600-mile convoy, gives me something to be tired about. Oh yeah, the convoy came through without a hitch. Captain Strader seemed tickled to death that we handled it so well. I breathed a sigh of relief when we rolled in here tonight... We will probably leave for the field on Saturday noon. I'll try to write you tomorrow night... I really miss you. I hope you are doing alright; I hate for you to be up there all this time by yourself... I sure will be glad to get back home with you.

All My Love, Bob

August 8, 1941
Daisy in Chester

Hey My Own Darling Husband,

I enjoyed your letter and wish I could be with you. I'm really going to be a much nicer person to live with in Oct. I know I haven't treated you right, Darling. I'm truly sorry. Mother's leg has been bad again, so I've taken over the house. The wood stove is really the devil to cook on, and try to keep the fire going at the same time.

It's hot as HELL here. The doctor said Daddy was in good shape... I am gaining too much weight. I'm glad you are swimming a lot. There are going to be 100,000 troops stationed around Chester and the neighboring counties. Dad is about to have a fit... Wish I could sleep with you...

Aug 9, 1941
Bob in Lake Charles, La.

Hey My Dearest Darling Wife,

I am so sorry I did not write sooner; I miss you something terrible. Every time I have a minute to myself, I think back to how wonderful it was when I could go home every night and be with you. Today, when I laid down after lunch for a nap, I thought of the many times I have seen you undress and go to bed with me. I wanted to be with you like that so bad I had to get up and walk around. I have the greatest desire to be with you and sleep in your arms tonight. You are in my thoughts continuously, and when I get my mind off the worries out here, I find myself wishing I could be with you. Daisy, I will never be irritated or be cross at you again. If I am able to stand these two months away from you, I will never forget what it is to be without you. In your letter, you seemed just a little mad at me. I'll try to keep from making you feel like that. This is a hard life out here under the constant drubbing of the captain but that isn't going to worry me anymore. I have hit my stride and from now on, I will be able to take everything with my chin high and a smile on my face. I enjoyed your letter today lots. I am hoping to get a lot of them; it really helps me keep up out here. I have written you about six letters. . . Harry was reading Melba's letter today and suddenly emitted a deep groan, "Oh my gosh!" he said. "Melba has just bought a fur jacket for $125. " I think that is the first he had heard of it. I still haven't breathed a word of our purchase, and won't. I am anticipating a wonderful fall and winter with you. After these two months, we will deserve it. I haven't been doing a darn thing except playing poker. My total outside pleasures have been taking 3 men to the doctor, getting food out, and having mishaps on each outing. If you really don't need the dollar, I will put it on the grocery bill. Darling, if you ever need any money let me know, I will get it and it won't be any trouble at all. Darling I love you so much. Until the next letter, all my love for always,

Bob

Aug 10, 1941
Bob in Lake Charles

Hey My Darling Wife,

I liked your letter and hope to get many more. I'm sorry you don't have mine yet. It's a pleasure to write you every day. It means more to me since we are married—I feel like a loving husband. I have changed, and want to save money until I can spend it with you. . . I'm going fishing on Sunday. . .

Aug 15, 1941
Daisy in Chester

Sorry I haven't written you more. . . Mamie and R. C. rented an apt., bought a lot of furniture, and move in on Saturday! I miss being with you and making love. . . We have 1 1/2 months to go. I only have 3 cents left, and will buy a stamp. . . Darling, I don't feel as if I'm leading a normal life. I don't like it. Be careful, and all My Love for always, Me

Aug 18, 1941

I don't want you to feel sorry for yourself, but to have a better attitude. You struggled through college; I still want you to have grit and determination, to act like an officer. You're young at 23 and need to learn to take hard knocks. I know you won't like my saying these things, but I want to have confidence in you and be able to depend on you, not just on Mother and Dad. I'm pulling for you, but I can't do it alone...

Not dated, 1941
Bob in Lake Charles

Gosh that was some letter from you today, Darling. It kind of took my breath away, but I deserved it. Don't worry about me losing my confidence. No one else has ever heard me talk like that. It's only when I am going through a tough time, or living under a strain. I was almost snowed under when I wrote, but since then, I have my ego back, and I promise not to ever let myself get down like that again. From now on, it's chin high and take everything without a murmur. Your letter helped a lot. I didn't resent it a bit. In fact, I needed just that. Darling, I can hardly wait until we are together again. You will find that I will have a better slant on life. We are having a break now; won't go into action until Saturday or Sunday. This maneuver is a lot more fun than the last one. I am getting so I can talk to majors and colonels and not feel like a 2-cent piece. I'm proud of how our group did in a recent smoke detail. . . Don't ever think about an abortion—I will take care of you.

Aug 26, 1941
Daisy in Chester

Hey My Dearest Darling husband,

I miss you so dam much it's awful terrible. Vogue Furriers is asking for payment, or they will sell my coat. I wrote them a dam good letter...

Not dated
Jimmy (brother) to Bob

I can't lend you the money. I'm broke, and have so many expenses for my family...

Not dated
Bob to Daisy

I'm so happy we have lived together... Harry might get out of the Army, but now his family wants him to stay in... Please go on to Greenville and check on our fur coat...

Aug 27, 1941
Daisy in Chester

Enjoyed your letter so much. I miss you, my love, so much. Louise J. and I went around to see Isabel and the twins. She is terribly thin and worn out, but happy... Darling, all I do is worry. I know it's silly but I can't help it. I know you'll take care of us.

Won't you? We've got 41 long days until we're together again. Since you went to a dance, would you mind if I went to one for the soldiers in Chester? Mother says all men step out when their wives are away, and it shouldn't be one-sided... Jimmy & Sally are coming for the last week in Aug. Hate to see them after trying to borrow that $50... Know you must be terribly tired. Darling, do take care of yourself.

Not dated
Bob to Daisy

Hey My Darling Wife,

Receiving your letters is really a pleasure after four or five days out in the woods... I don't want you to worry about money; I've made arrangements to make payments... I have orders for another year of active duty, lasting until Nov 1942, and I hope to be a first Lt. by then. Our company "C" is the only one getting favorable comments, and I think we will be a battalion this winter... I am hurting that I can't see you... Darling, I don't mind your going to a dance. I know you love me and I would trust you anywhere. Needless to say, I would much rather be with you myself, and hate to think of anyone else holding my wife in his arms, even in dancing. Bye Darling.

All my love, your Bob

Aug 28, 1941
Daisy in Chester

Hey Dearest Darling Husband,

I'm sitting at the dining room table in your home with Alice. I sure wish you could be here with me. Darling, I want you so bad. It's awful. I wake up nearly every night to reach over and touch you and you're never there… It's raining here and real cool…

Sept 9, 1941
Bob in Lake Charles

Hey My Dearest Darling,

I was out on maneuvers the last two days… I want you so bad… Did you know I have grown a mustache? I may let you see it, then cut it off. I wouldn't like it all the time, but it's something to do out here. I am anxious to know if the money arrangements I made suit you. Let me know what you are going to do about the coat… Things in the company are going from bad to worse, but my morale is still of the highest. I am learning to take it day after day without a murmur…

I love you with all my heart.
Bob

> Sept 10, 1941
> Daisy in Greenville

I miss you so dam much I can hardly stand it. . . I came to Greenville on the bus, sat by Bobby L. He's going in the Army and will be sent to Harvard University for a course. Sissy is marrying a man from Texas. She has a big diamond and money to pay cash for everything. . . I have paid $20 on the fur coat. Time drags when I'm not with you. I hate to sleep without you. The children really have grown. Little Kirk talks a lot and he's so sweet. Kirk and Harriet's home is very pretty. Wish you were here with me. John [her brother] called last night & said for me to catch the bus right away for Charleston as Mary has had a nervous breakdown!

> Sept 13, 1941
> Daisy in Charleston, SC

We have been going out and drinking. Mary is just tired. . .

> Sept 21, 1941
> Daisy in Charleston

I'm afraid something will happen to you, and you won't come back to me. I couldn't go on living if you didn't. Please be careful- you're my whole life—won't you hurry home to me?

> Sept 22, 1941
> Daisy in Charleston

My Dearest Darling Husband,

I love you so much. . . Saturday night we went out with some Army Doctors and their wives. They're the craziest bunch of people I've ever seen. Last night we were out with the Navy. . . I've been going to the Officer's Club with Mary, to play bridge, and have a good time. Mary & John say they are going to adopt me! Everyone seems to think I'm so dam young to be "Mrs."! I don't. I'd rather be "Mrs. " than anything else in this world. I've got to go home sometime, but Mary & John don't want me to.

[A note enclosed from Eleanor: I know you are a "lost sheep" without Bob. . .]

Not dated
Bob to Daisy

Enclosed is an accounting of our expenses and payments—I have paid off our debts. . .

Sept, 1941
Daisy in Charleston

I'm leaving on the bus for Columbus (Ft. Benning). I have played bridge and been drinking quite a bit with a fast crowd. Mary plays a lot, stays up late and tries to keep up with John. I'm glad I don't live here. . . I love you. See you soon. . .

Oct 21, 1941
John Nixon Sr. in Chester to Daisy

Dear Sister,

Received your letter & think it was about time you were writing. I want to know how you are getting along, and want you to write me regularly... I have been trying to get some grain planted ever since you left, but the ground is too hard. Haven't had a drop of rain since you left... J. F. killed himself last night by shooting... He was buried this evening at 4 o'clock. Haven't had the details yet... Lots of the soldiers have moved on. Heard some were coming from Ft. Benning. Bob and his crowd are old campaigners by now, I suppose. I miss you being here, worrying and aggravating me. When are you coming back? I am not fooling. I want you to write me more often & tell me all the news. Love to you both. JNS

12/3/1941

[Saved by Daisy: Two typewritten pages from Major Strader, "Training program, December 1941, to Second Chemical Regiment, Company C, Fort Benning, Georgia".]

IV. 1942—Baby Makes Three

"I have become a two-woman man (you and Nikki).

~Bob, 11/30/1942

Jan. 10, 1942
John Nixon Sr., Chester to Daisy,
Columbus, Ga.

 I have been waiting day after day to hear from you. I can't understand what has gotten into you. You know perfectly well that I want to hear from you & there is no reason that you can't write at least once a week. You can show me this consideration. It is awful cold here today. Had a light snow last night... If you are not coming home soon, will send you a turkey. Your mother says she will cook it for you. Have had several rains so can't do anything much. Let me hear from you by return mail. Lots of love. How are Bob & the Battalion?
 JNS

Jan. 27, 1942

Dear Sister,
 Received your letter and was more than glad to hear from you. Wish I could come to see you for a day but just can't get off. Am trying to plow, as we have had a good long spell of clear weather. Know you are all on edge just waiting around. If you want to come home for a while, will be glad to send you the money & will be mighty glad to see you. Miss you a whole lot. It is sort of lonesome without you to fuss with. Don't see anyone, as everyone is staying at home saving tires. I was going to swap Dan [his horse] for a mule but I will have to keep him, as I will have to ride him to town. Don't worry about Bob's First Lieutenant, as it will come in good time. The government is the slowest thing I know. Pack up your stuff & send it to me... I will pack it away... Henry M. was turned down, account of his eyes. Lots of love and let me hear from you.
 JNS

Feb, 1942
R. C. Guy, Sr. [Bob's Dad] to him

It has been quite a time since we heard from you and think you might be in Japan. I would like very much for you to write us occasionally at any rate... We hear from Eleanor that John B. had his tonsils out and is doing fine... Give us an inkling of your plans... Tell me more about yourself and work...

I am yours, RC Guy

Feb. 16, 1942
JNS in Chester

Dear Sister,

I was glad to hear your voice. I was afraid you were sick. We can't understand why you don't write. You say you are not doing anything, so you ought to have plenty of time. I hope you have written the people I phoned you about. None of them understand why you haven't written... Isabel married one of the cavalry soldiers who was here on maneuvers. I think you met him... I suppose you heard that Johnny H. crashed Thursday night & both he and his instructor were killed. The funeral will be tomorrow morning at eleven o'clock. I will be one of the pallbearers, a very trying task... Your mother has a boil on her right arm, so don't know when she will write. It looks like it will be raining in the morning. Hope I won't catch cold...

Sorry to hear Bob has been sick. Hope he is ok now. Write and tell me about yourself, & what you are doing. Thank you for the valentines...

JNS

March 3, 1942
Bob at Ft Benning

Hey My Dearest Darling,

It feels so awful to write, instead of talking to you. Daisy, honestly, I am lost without you. Last night and yesterday, I felt as if I had lost an arm or something. It really feels like hell to live without you, after being with you so long. I still can't believe you are at home. I still think I will see you tomorrow night. Gosh, dear, I wish I could.

It is really tough living out here in a dam tent. It has rained and snowed off and on all day. I really miss having you to keep me warm.

How is that BOY? You better treat him right while I am not there to look after him...

Enjoy your visit while you have a chance. I am going to try to get a few days leave around the fifteenth. How was your trip home? I am anxiously awaiting a letter from you. I would like to hear what is going on at home. Everyone there is suddenly more important, now that you are there.

I love you so dam much, and I will write again soon.

All my love, Bob

March 6, 1942
Daisy in Chester

Something must be wrong (baby) with me, as cigs. make me feel sort of sick, but I wish you'd send me 1 carton & Dad 2. . .

Isn't this awful–[a friend] had a baby and died a horrible death. Went blind and had convulsions. She was completely all right before she went to the hospital...

A woman notary Republic married Isabel & Charley! Jane's giving a big reception Saturday night. Mamie and I are going to help... Write.

I want a hot date with my husband to-night... Daddy said our car is useless now. Please try to get something out of it right away... I hope you will come up on the train. I hate to think of you in a dam ole tent... I'm going to wear my red evening dress to-morrow to Isabel's Reception. It's getting right tight.

All My Love, Daisy

Not dated
Bob in El Paso

Hey My Darling Wife (pregnant),

I don't like being without you... Please sign the income tax form and send it... I am looking for a good room for us, better than the last place, and hope you can come next Saturday...

Not dated

Everything is all set. Just as soon as you finish your visit at home, I am all ready for you to come back. I took this afternoon off and went room hunting. I forgot to tell you that I borrowed sixty dollars from Mix and will pay it back May 1. I felt better when I was able to get some money for a room. It has kitchen privileges; I will meet the owner's wife next, and get the room if I think you will like her. The room was real nice, in a brick house, with venetian blinds, pretty curtains & hardwood floors. We can get maid service and all our linen furnished.

Darling, come back as soon as you have visited home long enough. I would be tickled to death if you came back Sunday or Monday, for I miss you so dam much. . .

April 3-6, 1942

[Melba Raysor drove with Daisy to El Paso, Texas, where their husbands were stationed at Ft. Bliss. Daisy sent postcards from the trip to her relatives.]

April 19, 1942
JNS and Daisy Hampton, Greenville

Dear Sister,

Glad you got to El Paso O. K. You must have had an interesting trip. Will be here some time, as I have to go to the Doctor every day & can't get this treatment at home. Feel fairly well but not like doing anything. Keep us in touch as to where you are, because you never can tell what will happen. Glad you have such a nice place to stay. Only wish I was out there. How is Bob, want you to take care of yourself & see a doctor when necessary. Will write you from time to time according to how I feel. The Doctor says the treatment is doing O. K. & I am improving so far. Wish I could see you. With lots of love, & best wishes.

Be sure to come straight home if Bob should have to move. JNS

Dear Daisy,

Dad was not feeling good. Lucius G. said Dad needed some treatment; Kirk brought us to stay with them. Otherwise, it would have cost so much to keep going back & forth. Have been over here two weeks & probably have 4 weeks longer. Dad has been so worried for none of us knew your address. . . People are beginning to plant cotton. . . We are glad you are so well fixed. You did not mention how much you had to pay for all those fine things. How does Bob like it out there? I hear that it gets 112 in daytime but cools off at night. Mary has been to El Paso—all through there. Kirk has quite a nice garden. Has built a chicken house & has game chickens. They have lots of young couples in neighborhood. . . I had to practically unpack your trunk looking for table things to send, but only found your big tablecloths and napkins. . . I certainly do hope by now you have been to the doctor Daisy, I have enough to worry about without you doing like you have. Dad says you have no right to worry him so. I don't know what we would do without K. He is right there when needed. He has to put up with us so long. Write them a note every now & then, for they have been good to us. I see by the paper that Bob's sister's baby has come. Be sure & start buying a few baby things all along, for they are getting so scarce, no little laces. I doubt whether I will have any extra money to send you now, as Dad's treatments are going to cost a lot.

Love, Mother

[Daisy's father was being given radium treatment for cancer of the tongue.]

Undated note
JNS to Daisy

Dear Sister,

I don't feel like writing much. Hope you are feeling OK & taking care of yourself. Am not feeling OK yet. Suppose it will be weeks before I can hope for much. Miss you a lot & wish I could see you. This treatment is the worst thing I have ever been up against. The pain is bad. Will go back to Greenville on May 5th for the day. K & Harriet did everything they could for me. Saw lots of their friends, but I can't do any talking much, as it makes my face hurt. Right now, it is full of radium which explodes every once in a while. Hope to be rid of it in another week or two. Then maybe I can get some peace. Lots of love

JNS

[*In May 1942, Bob went to Chemical Warfare School, Edgewood Arsenal, Md. ; Daisy stayed in El Paso.*]

May 5, 1942
Bob in Md.

I am so dam lonely tonight Darling, just to think that I have to live without you makes me sick. Even though I miss you like hell, it is better that you are still in El Paso for the housing situation is worse here than it was at Benning. One of the Battalion officers has only one room in Bel Air, about twenty miles away. I sure would hate to have you staying like that again.

Gee, Darling, I sure am glad we didn't give up that swell apartment. Here's hoping I get to stay there with you all summer. I hope I hear from you real soon. I am worried about you. Please write a lot. You know I have to hear from you a lot. Our first day of school was okay. I hope I don't get tired of it. Anyway, it is only for one month. . . I enjoyed seeing Jimmy, Sally and Skippy in Washington. . . I went by the Chief's office; promotions will be coming by the end of the month. My recommendation never got where it was supposed to go. I am glad that major is gone. He certainly messed everything up. Daisy, I love you and am so anxious to hear from you often. Please write me all about yourself. Bye Darling.

All my love Bob

May 4, 1942
Daisy in El Paso

Just finished reading your letter. I'm so glad you miss me. I love you. The Greens moved in Wed. morning. The Burns had me over for supper last night. He came for me & bought me back. They invited me to go to Carlsbad tomorrow. . . He got you for his Co. , but he's leaving for San Antonio to be stationed there. Isn't that terrible. . . Kirk called Tuesday to tell me that Dad has cancer of the tongue! He is taking Radium treatment for it. I cried & cried; they haven't told anyone at home. The treatment is severe and few people can take it. . .

May 7, 1942
Bob in Md.

I am terribly sorry to hear about Nick. Please don't worry too much. I sure wish I were there with you. If you want to go home, please go. I'll send you some money as soon as I get my mileage pay. . . I don't like being without you. I would rather have one night with you than a week in New York or Washington. I'm glad you're my wife and true love. How is that boy of ours? Let me know how he is getting on, and the first time you feel him kicking. It shouldn't be long now. I'm sorry that Capt. Burns was transferred, but that puts me one step nearer to having a company. . . I long for you every minute of the day.

May 12, 1942
Daisy in El Paso

I opened a charge account and got a beautiful pink coat & hat at a good price. Please send some cash so I can get maternity dresses. . . Darling, your baby is just bouncing around. It's a wonderful feeling. Please hurry home to me. I love you so much. You all are going on maneuvers in Aug. in Louisiana. . . I would like to have twins. . . The utility bill is not much. . .

May 13, 1942

I think I am having a boy because I can feel a fast heartbeat. I'm much bigger now. . .

May 15, 1942

I bought a blue maternity dress... Col. Stark told Capt. Burns that you are one of the best and hardest working of his men, and you are doing Captain's work...

May, 1942
Bob in Md

I feel much better now that this month away from you is almost over. I want to see you so bad that I am just in a fog. Nothing seems real. It seems like a horrible dream, and I wake only when I see you again. We had a night problem last night. Our schoolwork is almost over—I don't know how much I have learned, but I am thinking along new lines. I have my ambition up again. It will be such a pleasure to go back to work for Col. Stark. All the fellows in school are beginning to get their orders and "sweat 'em out. " Darling, I am anxious to see how you are holding up. Are you gaining any weight? Of course, I know you are, but how much? I hope you are eating good and varied food. For gosh sakes do everything to make our baby the best in the world. I know he is going to be anyway. Please put Lt. Hoffman on the waiting list for housing. His wife is nice; I knew them in Columbus... Please take it easy and don't hurt yourself. I will be so relieved to get back to you.

May 16, 1942
Bob in Md.

Hey My Dearest Wife,

I have been to the Officers Club tonight and had a couple of

Scotches so I feel pretty good. I sure could go for you tonight. I am glad we are happily married...

Every woman I played bridge with tonight was talking about her kids. I am really proud that ours is on the way. Don't hurt yourself and take it easy. I have only two more weeks here. I won the high score prize tonight... I am making a lot of contacts now. I hope they will do me some good... I can't even breathe without thinking of you.

All my love to you and ours, Your Bob

May 19, 1942

I enjoyed your letter today and I am so glad you are finding something to entertain you. I would hate to think of you down there with nothing to do... Daisy, I am so dam tired of living without you. I am leaving here on the 30th and hope to be in El Paso on the 2nd. I will let you know later on. I miss you worse than ever before. Last night, I couldn't sleep for wanting you, and I constantly dream about you...

May 22, 1942

I feel good after playing tennis. I'm glad about the boy, and how nice you are getting along. It really thrills me when you write about the kid turning over. Is he really moving? I can hardly believe I am going to be a father, but I really like the idea. It means so much to me that you are taking everything so good. I can hardly wait to get back. I think about it all day long. We are moving along pretty fast, and it won't be long until I am happy once again. I'm so lucky to have you; our love will get bigger and bigger.

May 28, 1942

By this time next week, I will be about home. Won't that be swell... I will have an all-night problem tomorrow; then, I am ready to be with you. I told everybody in Washington good-by; I don't know when I'll see them again... I love you, Dear, for always. How's the boy?

July 24 & 25, 1942

[1 train ticket stub saved from El Paso to New Orleans. Daisy went to Chester to help take care of her father, who was sick with cancer.]

Not dated
Bob to Daisy

I miss you, and wish I had not let you go home. I'm hoping the Battalion will get sent to the Carolinas... It's hard for me to do work without you here... How is the baby?

Not dated
Bob in Louisiana

Hey My Dearest Darling,

I hope you reached home safely. Let me know how everything is. I wish I could have gone with you. I hate to leave you alone for so long. You have so dam much on your shoulders the next few months. I cleaned up the apartment and checked out Monday. I'm sending you the $15 deposit. Our bank balance is $454. 58. . . I want to apologize for the way I acted last night. I know that it wasn't your fault but I just couldn't take it. I felt so dam bad about your going away that I nearly went crazy waiting for you that night. Darling, forget that night and remember all those others we spent together. I want you to take good care of yourself at home. I feel like hell and so dam helpless way down here where I can't do a thing. Write me a lot. I am anxious as hell about you. When I don't hear from you, I can imagine all sorts of things. We had a successful trip here; everything went off swell. We are now in bivouac close to Mansfield, La. We will probably leave here sometime next week. Darling, I love you more than ever before. Give my love to your folks, and take care of yourself and our boy. . .

Aug 11, 1942

Things have settled down, so I can think of you and dream about seeing you again. I have a swell time remembering how much I have enjoyed my life with you, and thinking about when we will be together again. My love for you keeps growing and growing. When I see you again, I want to stay right with you for days and days. I won't ever get enough of just being near you. I still have thirty dollars so I won't need anything more for a while. . . We are starting another problem today, and awaiting orders to move out. Maneuvers this summer are a hell of a sight tougher than last year, but I won't have any trouble. . . Daisy, my radio is really a comfort. It's a pleasure to get some good music out here in the woods. . .

What Doctor are you going to see? I wish you would go ahead and have the baby somewhere besides Chester. If you can't arrange it, I'll come home and fix it myself. Write me all about how that boy is doing. Is he still kicking?

All my love, Bob

Aug 13, 1942

Hey My Dearest Darling,

I wish I could be there to help you. It is mighty cruel that I won't get to be with you all the time while you are pregnant. Daisy, I wouldn't take anything in the world for Buster. I realize how lucky I am, even though I don't get to be with you. We had an experience last night. Lt. Estes, Lt. Arner and I drove across the country to get a bottle of beer. Coming back, the truck stopped. We had to walk seven miles to camp, then go back and pull it in. Glad Major Strader wasn't in command to raise hell about it. 'A' company gets along with each other, but not with Headquarters. . . 'A' company is showing up better than the other ones. Colonel S. really likes my kitchen. None of us have had dysentery like the others. I haven't been drinking much. . . Part of my life is missing without you. . . I am writing to you on a card table that we carry in our orderly room trailer. We are about 2 miles off the highway in the woods. All the boys were out last night, so everybody is sleeping it off this morning. The dam yellow jackets are all over this place. They won't even let you eat your food. . . I'm thankful for a good kitchen crew and real good food. It took a while to get used to Army chow after eating your cooking for so long. . . I hope Nick gets better. . .

Aug 17, 1942
Bob in Natchitoches, La.

Hey My Dearest Darling,

This is the first time I have had time to stop since I wrote you last. Another phase of the maneuver is over and we will rest until Monday. I wanted to write you yesterday, but I was marching the Co. to the front just about all day. Daisy, you must get someone to help take care of Nick. Honestly, Darling, I am so afraid something will happen to you and the baby. Please take care of yourself. I couldn't bear it if something should happen to you... I won't write much today for I have to pick up the boys' laundry this afternoon... Daisy, I miss you so much. I will just have to call you up tonight. Darling, when I hear your voice, I feel better right away.

All my love Bob

Not dated, 1942

I haven't been clean in so long that I hardly know how it would feel. I enjoyed my talk with you so much that I am going to do it again. It was a pleasure to hear your voice... I hope I can see you in September... Maneuvers this year are as bad as last year. Everything is all messed up, and we aren't doing anything except moving south all the time. Before long, we will be back where we were last summer...

Not dated, 1942

Darling,

Since I have gotten straightened out and will write regular, I expect you to keep it up too. That was a thrill to get two letters yesterday. I love you. I haven't been writing much because I have been so busy and it has taken me time to get used to the field again. I will write more often now. It was so hard for me to get over not being with you. There will be two or three days at a time, when we are fighting, that I may not be able to write, but I will as often as I can. Tonight, I kinda need consolation. There are so many things to think about when running an outfit. No wonder Capt. B. didn't click. But don't you worry, I can do it. I know that I am the best C. O. in this outfit and I intend for it to stay that way. Do you mind if I come and talk to you about all my troubles every day? It really helps out. I love you tonight. I am sitting on the back of a Command Car, writing, and haven't even gotten our guns or transportation. I am getting along swell with my company. We do the best we can with what we have. Raysor and I may make Captain. Gosh if I could get those twin bars I would feel like I was really doing something for you and the kid. I am going to try everything I can. At least when I leave you, I want you to have as much as possible for our boy. If I can up your allotment by fifty or seventy-five dollars, I will feel much better. I hope we will be back together in the fall; I couldn't bear it until I have a couple of months together with you and the kid...

In August 1942, Daisy was still in Chester, taking care of her father, while Bob was on training maneuvers in Louisiana.
The German army was advancing on Stalingrad, Russia. Gen. George Patton and others were planning military strategies with the British military. As many as 400,000 Jews were murdered in Nazi-occupied Europe.

Not dated, 1942
Bob at Camp Polk, La

Hey My Dearest Darling,

That telephone conversation with you yesterday was most enjoyable. I wish I could do it every night. It is like getting a new lease on life to talk to you. Honestly, I never knew that a person could care for anyone as much as I care for you. My love continues to grow each time I get a new thrill out of being married to you. I haven't known what love is until now. It is comforting to know that, even though the world is in turmoil, I have someone who will always be mine and someone I can love and look out for. Darling, don't worry about the future. We probably will have some tough times, but we'll make it okay.

Estes and I didn't like how Bischoff and his wife Doris acted when they were sitting on a blanket out in the bivouac area in front of the men. . . It might cause trouble with Col. S. Daisy, I can't make any definite plans about coming home because I have no idea of what we are going to do. I am going to try to come soon after the baby is born. . .

[There is an undated note, probably in 1943, from Doris & George Bischoff, thanking Daisy for flowers she sent when their baby Dorothy died.]

Aug 23, 1942
Bob in Leesville, La.

Be brave; I wish I could be there to help. . .

Aug 29, 1942
Audrey Hoffman in Oregon

Your Daddy's spunk is just what might conquer his illness. Do hope he is better now and tell me when you write. Buster's name better be changed to Beulah, with all those fancy clothes your mother is making. Maybe it won't be long until we can see the little rascal...

Sept 2, 1942
Bob in Leesville, La.

Hey My Dearest Darling,

I feel so bad about not writing you more often. Things have been happening so dam fast that I have hardly had time to think. We have been separated from our headquarters, so we don't get a chance to get mail off. Our tenth problem was over this morning. We will move to the Fourth Corps tomorrow and it doesn't look as if we will get any break... Darling, I wish these next six weeks were over so we could get together again. I am really looking forward to life with you and the kid this winter. It will be a new life for us, won't it? I am going to write more often. I know you need my letters. Bye Darling—

Undated, 1942

I am so worried that you will work and worry too much. Fenton said, if your blood pressure went up again, you should go to bed and rest a few days... Have you finally decided to go to the Chester Hospital? I wish there was somewhere else to go. I won't rest easy until you are in the hands of some competent obstetrician... I have been on the verge of coming home to see how things are getting on. I know you will do the right thing about our child and your family...

Sept 8, 1942

I feel like a new man now that I have seen you and know you will be in good care the next two months. I really enjoyed being with you. I know I was kinda restless, but it was like a dream to spend those days with you. I hate like hell to be away from you but there's nothing I can do about it...

Sept 14, 1942

I am in a bivouac area in Texas and am waiting for the kitchen truck to come back so I can get some chow. I am dam near sick. I got a hell of a cold last Problem and I am having a hard time keeping it under control...

Not dated
Bob in La.

I know it hurts to be hungry all the time, but you can do it... How much it will mean to us to have a family all our own. When I think of our having a little child to take care of, it makes me think that we are at last beginning to live. If this dam Army would just let us alone, we could really live, couldn't we? The company is doing a great job... Capt Love is trying to get home a few days to help when Mike has his tonsils out... My few days at home gave me a new lease on life...

Sept 16, 1942

I didn't realize you would weigh 200 lb but I guess the Doctor will make you lose some of that. Darling, I hate to think of you going hungry but it is the best thing. How are you and your mother getting along? I hope Kirk's children won't worry you too much. I got back to the company okay, and have really been having fun since then. One time I went across the lines on a commando raid, stayed all night and didn't get captured. For this last problem, we held up a whole armored division for almost two days. ... Please do what Dr. Fewell asks you to do...

Sept 21, 1942

It rained for almost two hours this afternoon. Nothing is worse than Louisiana in the rain. Now, the sun is shining, and I feel pretty good, as good as can be expected without you. Gee, Darling it would be so much fun to spend a weekend with you. I have been away from you too long. I wish I could get off these maneuvers. As I see it, we don't have enough equipment to do any good here, so we might just as well be on Post enjoying ourselves. Sometimes I think we are unlucky as hell to be just married and have to live under such trying conditions. It's hard as hell for me to be away from you just prior to the arrival of our first child. . . But it will be so wonderful to have someone to call our very own. How much fuller life will be when we have a little one that is part of both of us. I know the kid is going to look like you. I hope he is big, blond and husky.

Are you still going to name the girl John Nixon, if it's a girl? Darling, I couldn't tell whether you were fooling or not. If you really want it, it's alright with me, though I think it's giving the girl an unfair advantage at the start. I have always hated to see a girl with a boy's name. It just doesn't work out, and it makes the girl different from all her friends. When I was little, I used to hate my name like all thunder. Darling, I am not going to say any more on the subject but if you still want to name her John Nixon, I certainly will agree. I am hungry as hell tonight. Sure wish I could eat some of your good cooking. Yet, the food is usually good, because we have an excellent kitchen in 'A' Co. It seems ages since I heard from you last. I'm hoping for a letter. I hope I am with you this fall and winter. I would hate to miss those early months of our baby's life. I know that fathers always gripe about getting up every night but still they hold every moment of the time dear to their hearts. Darling, when the baby comes, don't worry about me not loving you any longer. You'll see, it will just bind our marriage and make it more secure. I love you more now than ever, and I know our love will grow stronger. Ours is no ordinary love. When I think of how much better you would feel if I were with you, it almost breaks my heart. Tell Nick not to worry. I'll be a captain soon. . .

Sept 26, 1942
Bob in Leesville La. (Camp Polk)

Hey My Dearest Darling,

Gosh it has been an awful long time since I heard from you. I don't know whether you have missed the change in APO, or whether you are mad at me for not writing. Honestly, Darling, I am on the go so dam much that I hardly have time to do anything. Lots of times, I stop and start a letter. I am going to write you more often if I possibly can, every other day. Are you losing any weight? I hope you can, so that you can at least eat enough to keep from starving... Lt. Mix has been married two weeks, and he sees his wife on weekends... It won't be long now. In October, you will be on the last lap. It seems cruel that I am so far away, but it's lucky that I am still in this country and have a dam good chance of seeing our baby. Do you think you are going to nurse the baby? If it is the best thing, I think you should. Whatever the Dr. says. Don't get disgusted this last month. I know it is hard but it will be worth it. I am beginning to feel like a proud father already. I hope nothing goes wrong. I am scared and will probably be a nervous wreck by the time the baby arrives...

Sept 29, 1942

I am taking time to write at the kitchen bivouac area, and it's hard, due to the cold. This weather will make a tough month; the company is fighting up in the front lines and I'm waiting to take food to them. I hope we'll finish today, so we can get some wool clothing before the men catch pneumonia. It's a pleasure to hear from you, Darling, when I am out in these dam woods. It sometimes helps me to keep going. When I hear from you, then I can look forward to the time when I can be with you again. I miss you like hell. I could get along better without an arm or a leg than I could being without you... If I sound a little blue, please don't feel bad about it. I will be all right. It's just that these maneuvers are about more than I can take right now. We've been fighting for three days. When we get a break, I will feel better. Please take care of yourself. I know you couldn't help falling but try to be as careful as you can.

Bye Darling—All my love for ever & ever, Bob

[Daisy's father Nick died August 26, 1942.]

By September, battles of World War II continued on many fronts. American Marines pushed back the Japanese on Guadalcanal in the Solomon Islands. The US deployed more troops to the Pacific Theater. Germany was fighting Russia at Stalingrad. By October, German General Rommel's minefields in North Africa failed to stop the Allied Armored forces—mainly British and European exiles.

Oct 6, 1942
Bob in La.

Hey My Dearest Darling,

Your last letter disturbed me so that I have to write before I go to sleep. I have returned from a 40-mile trip... I haven't had time to breathe, or sleep.

Darling, it's taking a lot of effort for me to write tonight. I am so worried about you. If you keep on like you are doing, something awful is going to happen. Daisy, you have got to snap out of it right away. I know that it is hard as hell for you to be pregnant and have so many other worries too, but you just can't let it get you down. Please for goodness sake try not to feel so dam bad about everything.

If it gets much worse, I will have to come home, for I can't stand it way down here in La. with you having such a hell of a time. Let my love make you strong enough to stand it. God knows I don't know how you can do it but you just have to. It broke my heart when I read your letter tonight... My hands are tied and I can't do a dam thing. All I can do is try to write and cheer you up, and I do that every possible chance I get. Darling, you have to do it by yourself...

> Not dated

I'm nervous as the time for the birth approaches. I wish I knew what was going on at home and how things are with you. The kid will probably be two days old before I find out a dam thing. Please wire me the minute you go to the hospital. I'll try to get there as soon as I possibly can. How is your mother doing? Start working on her to come with you as soon as you can stand the trip after I get back to the Post. Try to make her feel that we have to have her. Because we really need her with you for a month or so anyway. I don't know where we will go next, but imagine that it will be Ft. Bliss. Don't forget that I love you when you are having our baby. I know it will hurt like hell, but think how much it will mean to us. Wish I could be there in time to hold your hand.

All my love for always, Bob

> Oct 14, 1942
> Bob to Daisy

The Battalion is leaving on the 24th for El Paso. I am going to see that the train is loaded and then I am coming home. . . I can stay for 4 or 5 days before I head out for El Paso. . .

I was born on Nov. 4. Bob was present. Yes, I'm female, and named John Nixon, for my grandfather, who had died in August. I've always been called Nikki.

> Nov 6, 1942
> Jane D. [Isabel's mother], Chester,
> to Daisy, Greenville

Congratulations on the baby's birth—Nikki, Nov 4. I prayed that it would go well... Isabel and Charlie are living in New Jersey.

> Not dated
> Aunt Janie, Chester,
> to Daisy, Greenville

The news of your dear daughter's arrival made me very happy. I wish your father could have been here to welcome her... Certainly glad Uncle Sam realized the importance of this occasion and let Bob be present for the celebration... You will soon be astonished that you ever preferred a boy!

> Nov 11, 1942
> Bob at Ft. Bliss

Hey My Dearest Wife,

I arrived safe and sound Sunday night. I miss you... I wish we were enjoying Nikki's first few weeks together. I hated leaving you, but I'm thankful I was there to see you so happy, with our child beside you. Tell Harriet I appreciated staying with them... I put in for an apartment.

Bye Darling, I love you and our daughter. Bob (Papa)

November 17, 1942
Bob at Ft. Bliss, El Paso

Hey My Darling,

I imagine by this time that you are safely at home. I hope you are feeling better. Gosh, you must be awful weak. I wish there was something I could do to help you get well soon. I hope Nikki isn't being any trouble. Tell her to behave herself or I will tend to her the next time I see her. I want to hear from you as soon as you are able to write, for no one can tell me all about my daughter like her mother can. Darling, I like the idea of having a girl. Sure wish these next two months would hurry up and pass. It looks as if I am always wishing time would pass so we could be together again. Still, I am so thankful that everything is all over and both of you are fine. . . It's going to be awful hard for you to come out here before Christmas because the trains are really overloaded. I am not even planning to see you and Nikki until January. I am going to get a room downtown this week. Darling, I love you so dam much. Sure wish you didn't have to spend this time without me.

Bye Darling & say hello to Nikki.

All my love, Bob

Nov 19, 1942

I sure hope you and Nikki are all right. Darling, I know it is hard for you to write but I just want a little note from you telling me how you both are. I got to see her so little that I want to know if she is really healthy and in good shape. My knee is swelling up again and I am hopping around. . . One of the men has Scarlet Fever, so the company is quarantined for a week. No one can go on furlough. . . Intensive training is coming soon; I want to see you and Nikki again. However, if you come, you might have to turn around and go back. I hope for a few weeks together. . .

Not dated, 1942

Hey My Dearest Darling,

I received a letter from your mother again today. It certainly is nice of her to write me. I appreciate it a lot. Nikki must really be growing fast. You had better get your appetite back pretty soon so you will have enough milk for her. I hope she doesn't cause too much trouble. We are still quarantined but there is a good chance that the boy didn't have Scarlet Fever. Anyway, they say that his case has not developed any further, so maybe the quarantine will be lifted pretty soon.

Daisy are you doing alright financially? I still have some in our joint account in case you run short. It looks like our time is about to come but I don't believe we will go until next Spring. If they needed us now, we would already be on our way. I think it will be sometime in March. Daisy, how much does Nikki weigh? She should be growing right along now. I want a picture of you and her as soon as you are able to get outdoors. We are working hard now, trying to get all our firing done and finish our training. Lt. Arner came back married today; I haven't seen his wife but think she must be nice. Hoffman is in school in Leavenworth, Kansas. I am doing pretty well without you Darling. So, don't worry about me. I go to a show once in a while, and the rest of the time I spend sleeping and reading.

Nov 20, 1942
Bob in El Paso

The quarantine will lift next Saturday, and my knee is better. I'm glad you weren't here—didn't want Nikki exposed... I want you to come out the first week of January. The boy who had Scarlet fever died last night and they are making arrangements today... Everyone is getting married. Oh Darling, I am so dam glad that we got married when we did. I know you were awful young and it is going to be hard on you with the responsibility of a child to raise. But I'm so happy having a wife and daughter to love. I wouldn't take anything for you both. I want to work hard when I'm not with you to help all I can... It looks like we will play an important part in the war... I love you. Tell Nikki I said hello.

In November, 1942, the Allied invasion began in French North Africa—Morocco and Algeria. Germany invaded southern France. General Montgomery began a major British offensive on the Libya/Egypt border. By December, there was heavy fighting in Tunisia. Gasoline rationing began in the US.

Not dated, 1942
Bob to Daisy

I received another letter from your mother today. I sure appreciate her writing all about you. I hope you will be able to write soon. I haven't written more because I'm so lonely without you. I don't want you to come too soon, as the trains are so crowded. You'll need a reservation all the way through to El Paso. Have the man get the reservations via New Orleans and take the Pullman... I'd rather you would fly... I want to meet the Presbyterian pastor and have Nikki christened when you come.

Nov 23, 1942

Hey My Dearest Darling,

The quarantine lifted today so everything is back to normal again. I got a room in town near where we need to live. The post is too crowded. I hope Nikki is getting along all right. Make a snapshot of her and you, and send it to me...

Nov 24, 1942
Bob in El Paso

Hey My Dearest Darling,

I love you so much tonight, Dear, that it hurts. I never believed when I first met you that I would ever care for you as I do now. In fact, I never knew or could imagine how it feels to love someone as much as I do you. Do you remember how you used to say you didn't want me to stop loving you after the baby was born? Darling, I will never do that. I have a special place in my heart for Nikki, but she is just something that has been given me to love while I still am going all out over you. Daisy, I'll remember Nikki as I saw her at your breast that last afternoon. Darling, I never will forget that picture. It is embedded in my heart forever. But, when I think of you, I remember how full of happiness I am with you and how meaningless life is without you. Daisy, here I am writing like a schoolboy to his first love. I hope you don't mind. I can't forget how happy you were when I left you. I feel like a heel not being there to take my share of raising Nikki. But I'll make up for it, Darling, when we get back together again. By the way, it looks like we will be leaving soon. I can't tell whether it will be the 1st of January or February, or that we might leave Bliss before Christmas and go to a staging area. Dear, if I were you, I wouldn't plan on coming out here for we won't have any time together and it will be so hard on you and Nikki. Anyway, I am so thankful to have been able to be with you when Nikki was born; I will gladly go with that picture in my mind. Daisy, I can't help being a sentimental old fool. I love you so much. We are officially going on the alert the 1st of December. That doesn't mean anything but you can't tell what will happen these days... It's Thanksgiving Day. I don't have any complaints-actually I would give anything to be with you but there are so many things to be thankful for that one just has to bear all those things, Darling. I am just snatching time today to wish you a happy Thanksgiving and hope you and Nikki are both fine. I love you.

All my love, Bob

Nov. 30, 1942
Bob in El Paso

Hey My Dearest Darling,

What a thrill I got when I received the first letter from you Friday! It was just like coming back to life again. Then today I received another letter, and it seems like old times. Darling, I feel so close to you today that I am going to call you this afternoon. If I can just talk to you, I think I will be able to stand it. Daisy, I think you should fly out. It is just as safe as the train and is a hell of a lot less trouble. If you can make it before Christmas, I would be tickled to death. I hope you will be available when I call this afternoon. Lt. Ensley and I went out last night for a steak, and ended up at the Club. Darling, life is certainly a bore without you. I danced with two women; both were dates of officers in the Battalion. Mostly I just sat around, drank, and shot Bull. It looks like your Robert has definitely become a two-woman man (you and Nikki). I couldn't fit in anyone else if I wanted to. That's what love will do to you. Honestly, I am so much in love with you that every other woman seems dull by comparison. . . I wish I could see you and Nikki now. Why not plan to fly out as soon as Dr. Fewell will let you go? PS The officers of the Battalion presented Nixon (Nikki) with a silver cup. I will send it on.

Not dated, 1942

I have just finished a note to Kirk & Harriet. Sorry it was so late. Say, Darling, you give me hope today. Do you really think you could get out here before Christmas? That would be wonderful. I'll have you a nice place all fixed up. . . I enjoyed your two letters today and Darling, I really eat up every word. It is not often that a man has such an adorable family to love. Now that we have Nikki, I wouldn't trade her for a boy for anything. It seems as if I always knew she would be a she. . .

I am spending 12-14 hours a day on the Rifle Range, and developing into a good shot. . .

All my love, Bob

(Telegram) DEC. 6, 1942 DAISY TO BOB

DEAREST DARLING I WISH I COULD BE WITH YOU ON OUR SECOND ANNIVERSARY BUT IT IS IMPOSSIBLE NIKKI AND I ARE FLYING OUT WEEK AFTER NEXT LOVE = DAISY

Dec 7, 1942
Bob at Fort Bliss

Happy Anniversary! I'm enclosing presents and Nikki's cup...

I have completed 5 days on the Rifle Range... I hope that we won't have to spend any more of our future anniversaries apart. How is Nikki? All my love, Darling,

Bob

Dec. 9, 1942

Hey My Dearest Darling,

It seems as if all the news has run out. Honestly Darling, I won't feel like doing a dam thing until I see you again. I miss you so much and wish I didn't have to come home at night and wonder if I could stand one more night without you... Nikki must be wonderful to be with. I know babies are a lot of trouble but when they are your own, then all the trouble in the world is not too much. I will gladly spend my nights walking the floor just to be with you. I have been trying to do some Christmas shopping, and it is almost impossible. This afternoon, I had to go out and observe a problem. Thursday, Friday and Sunday, we have Field Problems with our mortars and goodness knows what else next week. Daisy, bring an alarm clock with you if you have one. They are impossible to get out here. I am healthy and happy after a fashion, but won't be satisfied until I am with you again. Being with you means so much to me. I don't give a dam when you are not here to give me strength. Things don't go right at the Post unless I see you now and then.

Darling, I love you.

Dec 10, 1942

Hearing your voice today was worth a thousand times what it cost me to call. It made me feel good again. . . . I can't wait for you to get out here. I'll bet Nikki won't even know me. . . . I'm worried about you coming out all by yourself. Can you get a maid to come and help?

(TELEGRAM) DEC 11, 1942 DAISY IN GREENVILLE

START APARTMENT HUNTING AS NIKKI AND I ARE LEAVING WEDNESDAY IF OUR RESERVATION GOES THROUGH STOCK UP ON GROCERIES CANNED PET MILK AND WHITE KARO SYRUP WILL WIRE YOU WHEN WE LEAVE LOVE = DAISY

V. 1943—Far from Home

"I have seen enough of war now." (Bob, Aug 2, 1943)

In November, 1942, British and American troops made landings in French North Africa. In January, 1943, Winston Churchill and Franklin Roosevelt began meeting in Casablanca, Morocco. They resolved to concentrate first on efforts in the Mediterranean by launching an invasion of Sicily and the Italian mainland.
~Office of the Historian, US Department of State
In January, Britain was bombing Berlin. British forces captured Tripoli and Libya. The Soviets were fighting German troops around Stalingrad, and war continued with the Japanese in the Pacific.

Not dated, 1943
Bob, on training maneuvers Fla.

Hey My Dearest Darling,

We made our trip without incident and have been here since yesterday morning. This training is not as dangerous as I thought, so don't worry about me. I will be able to write often. . . Will probably come back to Bliss around March 10. . . Darling, I hope that when we get back, things will settle down so we can enjoy ourselves for another month or so. I hope you get something lined up on a house. We can move when I get back. I miss you so much. It is going to hurt when I have to leave you and Nikki to go overseas. We won't be going anytime soon; will probably stay here awhile. I am looking forward to being with you and Nikki. Are you taking your exercise course? I miss going home to you and Nikki every night. Write me once in a while, for I'm kinda worried about how you will make out there by yourself with Nikki. . . I am tired of being away from you, Darling. This trip didn't turn out like I thought and I have had enough. I will be dam glad to get back to El Paso. Would you let me know how you are? I hope you are not having a bad time of it. We haven't done anything to speak of the last two days. Yesterday, the fog was so bad we couldn't see 50 yards in any direction, and today it turned off real cold, with a high wind. How are the prospects for another place? This trip is almost useless. We are learning a few fundamentals, but it doesn't seem to be worth it. Darling, I am a dam sight better off in the 3rd under Col. Stark than I would be anywhere in the chemical warfare. I love you and am dying to see you and Nikki again.

Not dated, 1943

I am tired. I am glad this session is almost over. I have been ready to go back ever since I arrived at this dam place. It will be swell to see you and Nikki again. Ensley and I went out to Tallahassee last night and got stewed. It was the first time this trip, and it kinda lifted the tension. We have been satisfied with the set-up here, and all last week we just loafed around, couldn't do much on account of the weather. So, it was quite a relief to get out. We went to a nightclub on the edge of town. We spent the first part of the night just watching and having a few drinks. I certainly wanted you there with me. I have spent most of the time down here looking back on our few nights out together. One thing I want when I get back—for us to enjoy ourselves more. Back to last night, we had a big steak, and then I ran into a fellow from Spartanburg. He was about thirty-five and his wife about the same age. There were three couples of officers and wives, so we had a fairly good time from then on. We left about two and got back to camp about four thirty. Darling, every time I am away from you and go out, it makes me wonder how I ever enjoyed life before we were married. After knowing how much more fun it is to be out with someone you love, it is dead as hell to be without you. I expect to leave here on Wednesday. If you want to get in touch with me before I come home, call out to the battalion, and leave a message. One of my sergeants was hit by lightening Friday night. It was an unusual accident. He was asleep in his bunk and the bolt hit the roof, came down through a window, and hit a rifle leaning against the wall. It splintered the wood stock of the rifle and a part of the bolt jumped to his arm and flashed over his body burning him pretty bad in places. He is in the hospital, and getting along pretty good, but it will be a couple of weeks before he will be out again. I was dam glad that he wasn't killed. That would have been awful. It was bad enough to have him laid up like that. One of the Divisions lost some men in a landing operation.

It didn't affect my men. . . I don't want you to worry if you've heard about it. . . I'm looking forward to getting on the train and heading for home. Would you have a date with me on Saturday night? I sure would like a good steak with you and an evening of dancing. . .

Tell Nikki hello for me. . .

March 26, 1943
Daisy in El Paso

Dearest Mother,

Received your long letter today and enjoyed it a lot. Yes, Mother, I'm doing all my own work and washing Nikki's things. It's impossible to get anyone here; they come late in the morning, charge $2.00 and car fare, and can't speak English. Nikki is still sick, but much better than she was. She's wearing the dress you made & it fits fine. I wish you wouldn't bother to make her any clothes, as it's no telling when we will be home...

April 1, 1943
Bea (friend from El Paso), in Mass. to Daisy

I shouldn't be here—I should be your next-door neighbor forever. Honestly, Daisy, you'll never know how much I miss you... George is under a terrific strain—says he's losing his old self-confidence. He says the place is full of pigs, filth and mud. He's been promised a furlough at the end of maneuvers...

April 6, 1943
Bob in El Paso to Daisy's mother

Thank you for the money. We are glad to finally be living in a house where we have room to turn around without bumping into something. Nikki is really a swell daughter. I wouldn't take anything for her. I am certainly glad that I have had these last couple of months with her and Daisy. She is lots more than just a little baby. Already she has a personality of her own. She is beginning to sit up now with help. She can hold her head up real well. Tonight, Daisy and I let her sit up by herself on the sofa and she seemed to enjoy it so much... I am getting along fine, but just hope we get to stay here a little while longer...

April 17, 1943

["Certificate of Personal Property Shipped. "236 lbs from Ft Bliss, TX, to Chester, SC, by Robert A. Guy, due to "permanent change of station".]

April, 1943
Alice in Arkansas to Daisy

I wish we knew where the boys are... I had a rough trip to Ar. with the children... There are 30,000 troops in Tyler...

April 20, 1943
Bob to Daisy

(TELEGRAM)
EVERYTHING FINE.

April 23, 1943
Bob, North Africa

Hey My Dearest Darling,

I'm sorry I had to leave... The last few months were wonderful... Your letters will mean a lot to me.... Tell everyone hello.

Not dated

I got your letter and I'm glad you made it home safely. Write as often as you can; I enjoy hearing about what you are doing and how the folks like Nikki. I am wearing the money belt your mother gave me... Please send V-mails that get here faster... I miss you and Nikki; I'll be back sometime and then we can pick up where we left off.

All my love to you both, Bob

May 16, 1943
Bob to Daisy—V-mails

I am looking forward to my first letter from you... We are bivouacked on the side of a huge hill... I'm having trouble writing a good letter... Darling, write me about Nikki. How many teeth she has now, and the like... It is really hot. I have already blistered and started to peel. Maybe I can get a good tan soon...

May 22, 1943

Darling,

Don't worry about being put on the shelf. You just wait until I get back and there won't be any shelf... I don't have any use for money over here so I am sending all I can spare home in bonds...

May 25, 1943

It is Sunday in North Africa and I am going to church to keep contact... I am sorry that we didn't have Nikki christened yet... I'm glad everybody likes my daughter and that she is a sweet girl like her mother... I want you to have $300 or $400 in the bank for an emergency fund... I hope Kirk will keep the farm—we may want to live there someday... Tell that daughter of ours I love her very much...

May 29, 1943
Bob, North Africa

I wrote you while I was on the boat, but I don't think it was mailed right away... I am healthy and have more muscles. Sorry I missed your first Mother's Day...

May 31, 1943

I am writing to you by flashlight in my pup tent. Darling, it is really hard being so far from you and looking forward to something which I don't know what the results will be. We are finally reaching the test for which I have been preparing myself for the last two years. I have re-lived over and over every minute of our life together, and get all the strength I need to carry on from knowing that you and Nikki are waiting for me to come back, so that we can continue the happy life we have started. Over here, the troubles we had and all the worrying and waiting we did, have all vanished. What is left is a beautiful memory of two of the happiest years of my life, and a future promise of life together, which I will go through anything to attain. Keep pulling for me... I haven't had a letter in ages from you. Could you write me once a week, whether you hear from me or not? How is Nikki; I'll bet she misses her daddy. Don't you let her forget me, for I don't want to be a stranger when I get back.

1943—Far from Home

June 4, 1943
Alma, W. Va. to Daisy, Chester

Your letter was the first from the friends in El Paso. I don't fit in here and miss talking with you... I heard from George that they are in N. Africa, living in tents, and the weather is like El Paso. I was relieved that they had landed...

[From 1943 to 1944, other Army wives correspond with Daisy. They write about their children, and life without their husbands. They miss the good times together. An undated letter from Doris and George in San Antonio, tells about the death of their baby Dorothy—cause unexplained.]

The North Africa campaign began in June 1940, and continued for three years, as Axis and Allied forces pushed each other back and forth across the desert [Egypt and Libya]... In May 1943, thousands of British and American forces joined the battles, eventually helping force the surrender of all remaining German and Italian troops in Tunisia, thus ending the campaign. More than 250,000 prisoners were taken.
~The Atlantic, World War II, North African Campaign]

June 5, 1943
Bob, North Africa

Hey My Dearest Darling, I have finished reading two letters from you: May 13 and 15. You will get some from me soon; the mail station takes a long time... I miss you and Nikki. I am sending a check from Ciba, and hope you will buy a war bond to add to our fund...

June 6, 1943

I am glad Nikki is okay. My heart swells with pride every time I hear that someone said something nice about her. Darling, she certainly is a wonderful child. Next to you, she comes first. Be brave and remember I'll always love you...

June 7, 1943

There are times when I won't be able to write, but don't worry... I was really hurting when I left you at Fort Bliss, but I didn't want our goodbyes to be hard on you... I would give anything for this war to be over... Tell me more about Nikki. I won't ever get tired of hearing about her...

June 15, 1943

I have seen quite a bit of North Africa now and wish this thing were over so I could be with you and Nikki again. I am doing fine and in very good health, but my heart is broken. I don't know how long I can continue to stand this separation from you. I love you Darling and wish we were together again. I haven't received a letter from you in ages. Your last letter was May 15. I am aching to hear from you. How is Nikki? I love you always and forever...

June 18, 1943

I have been traveling and have seen some beautiful country. I hope the next time I see it will be as a tourist... Did you get the $100 war bond and the check? The mail is very slow... Be careful, and kiss Nikki for me.

June 21, 1943

Hey My Dearest Darling,

Are you getting my letters? I wish you would write as often as you can, for it is a hard life over here and letters from you are about all I have to keep me going... Please keep my family informed... May God be with you and Nikki.

I love you both...

```
June 23, 1943
TELEGRAM
ALL WELL AND SAFE. MY THOUGHTS ARE
WITH YOU. ALL MY LOVE-
```

June 27, 1943

I'm getting your letters now...

June 30, 1943

I love you my darling wife. Kiss Nikki for me. I feel like trying to tell you how much I miss you and long to be back home again. It is a hard job, to be over here facing God only knows what, so far away from you and not knowing when I will be with you again. It is the hardest thing I have ever tackled. I may not write much, and you may think that I enjoy it over here, but it is really hell. I would give anything in the world to have this all over and to be back with you again. The happiest part of my life has been the time that we were together. It was the only time in my life that I have known real happiness. I hate that we have had to go through all this, but it is a job that has to be done. Darling, when this is all over, I am going to spend the rest of my life making you and Nikki happy and enjoying life myself. I love you with all my heart. Even when I am working my head off over here, I still am thinking of you. Let this letter be a comfort to you and help keep your spirits up until I can get back. I will be doing all in my power to finish this job over here, so I can be free to live the rest of my life with you. I am still looking forward to receiving those pictures of Nikki. Daisy, I realize that the Army took a large part of me, and after this is over, you will have all of me again. Darling, I think a lot differently over here. Everything seems so much clearer. I don't want anything above the average life. I just want a chance to live with you and my children. People that go through life, without ever facing anything, never know what it means to live a normal life. I hope this letter makes you feel good. I try to help you stand this separation so that you can take good care of yourself and Nikki. Bye Darling

All my love is yours forever, Bob

July 2, 1943

Audrey Hoffman, Alma Arner and Peg Erwin are pregnant. I'm glad that Nikki was born before I left. . .

July 2, 1943
Isabel in Spokane to Daisy in Chester

Charlie has been very sick in the hospital with asthma. . .

July 4, 1943
Bob to Daisy

I have been thinking about Nikki all day. I wish I could see her now. She must really be growing up. I am still waiting for those pictures. It takes such a long time for letters to reach me here.

July 6, 1943

I was overjoyed to get the pictures of you and Nikki. Thank goodness, I have them with me. I like the one in which you have Nikki sitting in your lap, for there I can see both of my loved ones in one picture. The other two are real good of Nikki. Especially the one in the high chair. She has grown so much that I hardly knew her. I will carry these pictures over my heart, and that will help me get back to you safely. . . I really know what true love means now. Tell your mother hello, and all our friends around Chester. . .

July 16, 1943 Alma to Daisy

The Sicily invasion scares me, but I'm glad it's started, so it will be over sooner... I hope our boys don't get in it for a long time...

July 23, 1943
Bob in Sicily to Daisy

I am still alive and happy. I know you will be relieved... Tell everyone at home I am well and okay and doing just what I came over to do... I like Nikki's picture. Kiss her one time for me...

August 2, 1943

Please send cigarettes, candy, gum and v-mail... You sounded unhappy in your last letter. Don't let the little things get you down; get someone to look after Nikki so that you and your mother can go somewhere... I miss you so much it hurts all the time... I would like you to send me the Chester News... I want to get home and entertain my daughter... I was in the Sicily invasion, and I have seen enough of war now...

The Allies' Italian Campaign began with the invasion of Sicily on July 10, 1943. Combined air and sea landings involved 150,000 troops, 3,000 ships and 4,000 aircraft. Gen. George Patton commanded American ground forces. After 38 days of fighting, the U. S. and Great Britain successfully drove German and Italian troops from Sicily. Mussolini was toppled from power in Italy on July 24, and the way was opened for the invasion of the Italian mainland.
~History. com, 2009

1943—Far from Home

The 3rd Chemical Battalion was first activated at Ft. Benning, GA in 1942. The Battalion's first campaign was an amphibious assault landing in Sicily in July 1943. They successfully accompanied the initial assault waves of three of the four landing teams of the 3rd Infantry Division and provided smoke screen/explosives. As the Sicilian campaign was triumphant, the 3rd Chemical Battalion continued missions in Italy from November 1943—January 1944 in preparation for the key Battle of Rome.
~Wood. Army. Mil 3rd Chemical Brigade History

August 4, 1943
Bob in Sicily

I'm ready to come home any time... Nikki is 9 months old today. I wish I could see her. Those snapshots are a treat for me and I look at them every day...

August 7, 1943

When I get home, I want to spend about five or seven days with you and Nikki completely away from everyone else. It would partly make up for the time I have had to spend away from you. I have felt like we were cheated in not having a honeymoon, and a short trip somewhere would really be nice...

August 13, 1943

I have received more snapshots of Nikki-at 6 ½ months and 8 months. I miss you both... I haven't seen a soul from home, except one man from York when I was in Africa...

August 17, 1943
Bob in Sicily to Daisy

Hey My Dearest Darling,

I'm taking time to write a long letter and put my heart on paper. Your letters keep me in good spirits, and seem to cut down the space between us. . . I am writing this in a house that we are living in temporarily. No one else lives here, and we moved our beds inside to get off the ground. I am writing by the light of an old lamp. It goes out once in a while, but by a little shaking it burns again. . . I'll tell you more about this country when I return. I have seen a lot of Africa including Oran, Tunis, and Bizerte, and I have now seen most of Sicily. . . I imagine that you are getting letters from me again. I hated to have that long break, but during that time in July when I wasn't able to write, we were in the campaign and there was no mail service at all. As the fighting progressed, we were able to get a few letters out. I hope you got them right away. I love you more than ever. I can't understand how people can be married and not love each other. There's no one on this earth that I would rather have as my wife than you. I want to spend part of every day at home with you, watch Nikki and play with her, so she would know her daddy and mother were together. I don't want to spend time chasing a pot of gold. All I have been through has made me more appreciative of things at home; my love for you has grown accordingly. . . I'm not sure what I will do when I get out. Do you want me to farm, be a professional man, or be in the Army? If I could be with you tonight, I would never leave you again. . .

August 19, 1943

I want to settle down in Chester and farm or get an interest in things around there. I wouldn't like the competition of industry... Maybe I could make a good living at home and be a lot happier...

August 23, 1943

I am still in Sicily and unable to write much about what I am doing... Every day that goes by puts me closer to seeing you. I love you Daisy. Nikki must be really a big girl now. I sure would like to see her once again...

August 29, 1943

Wish you were here with me; I have been going swimming twice a day in the Mediterranean. This country is really pretty. I am in excellent health and doing fine, but still longing to be with you and Nikki. Send her snapshots by air mail so I will get them faster; I spend a lot of time looking at your pictures...

Sept 3, 1943
Alma to Daisy

I was worried about that darn Sicilian campaign. Today I get the news of the invasion of Italy, so I suppose it means more worries. I wish they would all quit right now—don't you? What will we get our husbands for Christmas?

Sept 3, 1943
Bob to Daisy

I was really thunderstruck to hear that Buck had been killed. I can hardly realize that he won't be home when I get back. Let me hear how it happened...

Sept 4, 1943

I'm very thankful for your letters—I couldn't stand it without you and Nikki to live for. I can't believe she's 10 months old today; I'm going to write her a letter on her birthday. When she's old enough, she will enjoy reading it...

Sept 5, 1943

I have been to church and will go swimming this afternoon... We had a battalion show last night and it was good, with satire and a good orchestra...

Sept 7, 1943

I'm glad Nikki is healthy; I felt sorry for her when she was sick in El Paso... I enjoy remembering our good times together, and I look forward to our future happiness... I send oceans of love to my wife and daughter...

Sept 12, 1943

In reply to your question about Christmas, I could use a watch, a hunting knife with sheath, and a small colored photograph of you and Nikki. I most want to be with you, but I can't depend on that. It seems so long that we have been apart.

Sept 14, 1943
Isabel in Denver to Daisy

Charlie has been retired from the Army and we are on our way East. We will see you and Nikki in about a month...

Sept 15, 1943
Bob to Daisy

I have been thinking about you lately Darling. I even had a long dream in which I was with you again. I am so dam tired of going on day after day with no hopes of seeing you soon. The news over here is good, but it is still going to be a long time before I see you again. I swim now and then, and have seen some pretty good USO stage shows. I hate to miss Christmas with you... Please send candy and cigarettes...

Sept 19-25, 1943

I never want to be separated from you again. Life is too short to spend most of it loving you from a distance... Dada thinks Nikki looks something like me... It is a pleasure to get mail from you. I'm sorry for the times when my letters don't get out regularly. I'm hoping for a miracle soon, to allow me to get back to you... It's hot, the mail hasn't come, and I don't feel well... I need you...

"The front-line soldier I knew lived for months like an animal, and was a veteran in the cruel, fierce world of death. Everything was abnormal and unstable in his life. He was filthy dirty, ate if and when, slept on a hard ground without cover. His clothes were greasy and he lived in a constant haze of dust, pestered by flies and heat, moving constantly, deprived of all the things that once meant stability—things such as walls, chairs, floors, windows, faucets, shelves, Coca-Colas and the little matter of knowing that he would go to bed at night in the same place he had left in the morning."
~Pg. 3, Chapter 1, "Prelude to Invasion (Sicily)" in Brave Men by Ernie Pyle. Scripps-Howard Newspaper Alliance, 1943, 1944, and republished 1978. Aeonian Press Inc., Mattituck, NY 11952

Sept 30, 1943
Bob to Daisy

I know that you miss me but I still like to hear about it. Please mix up your airmails with v-mails that come through much faster... I am so glad that we were able to get married when we did. I have so many pleasant memories... Sure would like to see Nikki. I never will forget those months we three spent together in El Paso. I'll always remember those nights when sometimes I would awake and feel you next to me, and hear Nikki sleeping in her crib. That is the real happiness to be found in life. I don't enjoy money or spending it, but as long as I have enough to provide for my family then I am not going to be bothered about other things. Just to have all this mess cleared up and to be able to live my life with you and our children. I've asked God for a chance to live the rest of my life with my family... Could our next be a boy? I would like it... I have often thought about our love affair. The first time I saw you that afternoon when you rode through Lowrys in the Darby's car, I was a marked man. On our first date, as I went down that walk with you on my arm, I should have known then that you were right where you belong, at my side... Until I am with you again, remember that I love you...

Oct 6, 1943
John, Fla. to Daisy, Chester

Dearest Sister,

Here's hoping this letter finds you, & Mother & that beautiful Nikki, O. K. She is the only baby I've ever really wanted... I am busy and like my life... Keep your chin up...

Oct 5, 1943
Bob in Sicily to Daisy

... You're the only woman for me, no matter how long I stay over here. Our life together is more important than anything else. I'm reminding you that I intend to come back... Please send cigarettes, candy, gum and pictures...

Oct 6, 1943

Enclosed are two pictures of me; they are not good, but the best I could do. Don't scare Nikki with them...

Oct 8-9, 1943

Your letters make a blue day bright... It looks like we have a lot of dark days ahead, but when it is all over, we will enjoy the happiness that should be ours. I would sure like to see Nikki. I'm glad people like her... I wish I could be with you this winter. I listened to the Notre Dame-Michigan game today. I'm homesick.

Oct 11, 1943

The moon is very beautiful here in Sicily tonight. I have spent the last hour watching it, and thinking how wonderful it would be if I could watch that old Carolina moon with you. I don't want you to worry about me for I am well and will be able to manage okay, except that I am awfully unhappy. To be here, where I never get to see you, or touch you, is actually torture. It takes me back to the year and a half I spent in New York. I don't mind being overseas so much, it is just that I can't live without you, Darling. My love for you has increased one-hundred-fold since I left you in El Paso. The weather has changed and we have a lot of rain and clouds. I can see a huge mountain, with the top in fuzzy clouds, a full moon shining above, the broad expanse of a plain reaching down to white tops of waves lapping the sandy shoreline, and on out to a vast expanse of the Mediterranean. It makes you forget your troubles and what's ahead. It makes you think of the ones you love and makes you feel closer to them. It makes you think of God and what little control we have over things. Darling, I now realize what it means to be an American, and to love someone more than anything else in the world. Whenever this is all over, we will find a true happiness together. I sent your Christmas box today. Hope you got it okay. We had communion services

Sunday. It meant more to me this time than it ever has before. Darling, I have learned to look to God a lot more often in the last six months. Whenever anything gets unbearable, I go off somewhere alone, think of God, and offer a prayer that everything will turn out all right for us. Then I think a lot about you and Nikki and I always feel better, and once again able to keep going. Darling, I love you with all my heart and always will.

Oct 13, 1943
Bob to Miss John Nixon (Nikki)
"Somewhere in Sicily"

My Darling Daughter,

I am writing this letter as a present for you on your first birthday. . . I hope that when you grow older you will like to know how much I regret not being with you personally on your Birthday. I certainly hope and pray that I will be able to be with you on all of your Birthdays to come. It has been awfully hard to be away from you and Daisy for the past six months. However, I am very thankful that all three of us were together in El Paso. I have and will carry with me over here pleasant memories of those three months. Nikki, your daddy is real proud of you. All reports from Daisy say you are a real good baby and doing fine. . .

As long as you and Daisy are O. K., I will be able to stand this over here much better. Nikki, I know you won't ever be able to really understand what this war is all about and I hope that when you are able to understand this that the world will be at peace again. . . After this war, the world should be able to straighten itself out. The night is pretty over here in Sicily. A full moon, hills, and the ocean really make a sense of grandeur. I spend a lot of time thinking of my family and looking forward to the time when we will all be together again. . . I hope you will enjoy having this letter written to you on your birthday. . . Your loving father, Bob

> Oct 14, 1943
> Bob to Daisy

I am enjoying American programs on the new radio. . .

> Oct 16, 1943

I got the cigarettes. . . Darling, I do so enjoy hearing about Nikki. Try to do the best you can about training her. It isn't good to let her get spoiled. . . I would gladly give up any more participation in this war just for you. . . The weather is getting bad and it looks like we will have a bad winter. . . I love you and want you so bad. . .

> Oct 18, 1943

Tonight, I took one look at the moon and one look at your picture and decided to write you before I went to sleep. Darling, that little girl of ours is really tall, isn't she? She will probably be as tall as you are. I am getting inspired about her hair. Do you think she will grow more? It seems to be kinda bald on the sides. Daisy, I miss you something awful. I left just about all of my life with you back in the States. This thing over here is just something to be borne until I can get back. . . The moon is perfectly beautiful tonight. The sea is quite calm and the moonlight seems to shimmer over the water. It brings back memories of the good times we used to have together. I was astounded by the number of men in the company whose best girls got married on them. That must be awful. I couldn't stand it if I lost you. One poor guy has lost three girls in the last year. I always thought absence made the heart grow fonder, but I guess it has to be real love to stand the strain of a long time apart. Darling, a love like ours could never be changed by any separation. That year and a half in New York was a hard one for me. I felt hopeless, because it would be years before I could support you, and I was so afraid you would go for someone else. Sometimes I feel real sorry for anyone who is fighting a war and has no one outside of his family. No matter how tough the going is, I always think of you, and am able to stand it. Daisy, I hope you are not getting too bored with Chester. I especially don't want you to get down on life while I am gone. You seem to be doing okay from what I can tell of your picture. Darling, I want to live at Chester and farm, or do something where we can be happy and enjoy life. . . We can stay in the Army as long as I get my present salary. The battalion is the same. One of these days, I am going to get the hell out of it. The only thing that I would miss would be the men in the company that I have known for so long. I don't know what it would feel like to serve over a bunch of strangers. Here I feel right at home because I know dam near every man in the company. . . Every night I live over again those wonderful two years we had together. It seems so awfully long now, since I left you standing on the porch at Alice Love's. If I had it to do it over again, I don't believe I could leave you.

Give Nikki a hug for me. . .

Oct 20, 1943

I got the jigsaw puzzle and all the mail; it made me feel good... I just had a good breakfast of oatmeal, pancakes and pork sausage... I love you as much in the morning as at night. My morale is dam good now. I am still in fine health, and there is not much worrying me except that I would like to be with you again. I hate to miss Nikki's birthday, and want to be with you to celebrate our anniversary...

Oct 22, 1943

If I could be with you, I would make you forget these long six months we have been apart. Darling you have become my whole life... Remember me to your mother...

Oct 23, 1943

I look forward to being with my two girls and making up for lost time... How did Charlie [Isabel's husband] get his discharge? While there's still a job to be done, I can stand it...

Nov 2, 1943

I hope you haven't been worried for the last few days. I have missed you like hell, and am glad to be able to write again. As you have probably already guessed, I am now somewhere in Italy. I am still well and doing okay, except as the winter comes in, I miss you more and more... I will be thinking of you on the special days of yours and Nikki's birthdays, our anniversary, and Christmas...

Nov 9, 1943

It is tough going over here and I thank my lucky stars that I have been preparing for this for over three years, for I am doing what I know how to do. Darling, I love you very much. It means so much to have you waiting for me. I think about you always Darling and it helps in a tight spot... When your letters finally reach me up here [in the mountains of Italy] after a hard day, all my worries seem to leave and I feel as if I could do almost anything. I find myself reading them over and over again. Please keep on writing and thanks for writing as much as you have...

Nov 18, 1943

I got the Christmas box and am enjoying the candy, cigarettes and gum... I miss you more in winter. How is Nikki? I love you Darling with all my heart...

November 23, 1943

Hey My Dearest Darling,

I had an urge tonight to write you a nice long letter. I am in a house for a few days and it is quite a pleasant change to hear the rain without getting out... I have been feeling awfully blue today. When I get time to sit and think, it almost gets me down. I guess it is a good thing that they keep us busy, for otherwise we would go crazy. I imagine that you feel the same way. This is awfully hard on both of us and I will be so dam glad when it is all over. It looks like a long time yet, but before we know it, I will be back with you again. I realize how lucky I am. A man is a dam fool not to find the right girl and get married as soon as he can. I don't see how a man can stand it without a wife at home to fight for. I know it makes all the difference in the world to me. Nothing is too hard to take as long as I know that you are waiting at home with open arms for me. It really hurts to think of how much you are missing me. I wish I could be with you tonight. I am sure we would be happier than we ever have before. I live over and over again those nights we spent together. If I could just feel you next to me once again, my happiness would be unlimited. Darling, don't get tired of waiting for me. Just think of the years to come when we can be together every night. I would really love to be able to walk in now and get acquainted with my daughter. Do you think Nikki will know me when I get back? She had better anyway. I'll bet I won't be able to take you in my arms at first because she will probably raise Cain. . . I received the letter with the pictures of you and Nikki. She sure has grown. You looked real pretty with your new permanent. Wish I could be there to mess it up for you. . . I was so glad to see that new permanent. I still want you to look pretty even though I am not there to see you. . . I don't need much money now, and would rather that you and Nikki have enough to carry in any emergency. Your idea for investing would be good.

All my love forever, Bob

Nov 25, 1943
Thanksgiving Day

Hey My Dearest Darling,

It is early on Thanksgiving morning, and I am attempting to convey my thoughts to you. I am going to church this morning to thank God for the blessings that I have received. I don't have to look very far to find something to be thankful for. Even though I am thousands of miles from home and my family, and in the midst of a terrible war, I don't feel cheated or down on my luck. I am very thankful to be alive and to be able to fight for my family and my country. I am thankful that I have found someone who is willing to go through life with me, even under the hardship of taking care of a baby girl, and keeping your spirits up so that I can feel that everything at home is all right. No fooling, Darling, it is wonderful to have your letters, full of good cheer and news about you and Nikki. I realize that you have troubles and probably sometimes feel awfully blue, but you never fail to cheer me up immensely. Remember all those tales about the woman behind the man? Well, as long as you are behind me, my road will always be easier. I am thankful that I had almost three years to train myself for this job over here. Even though those years were a lot of trouble for you and me, they were well worth it. I have been prepared for this war. Yesterday, I saw a man come in our infantry outfit as a replacement who has only been in the Army for four or five months. That must really be awful to go from civilian life to the midst of this war in such a short time. I hope you don't mind me writing so much. It isn't often that I am able to sit down like this and write at my leisure. The simple ways of life are more important when you can't have them. My wish for this day, more than anything else, would be to spend it with you and Nikki at home in Chester. What could be more simple, and so full of the joys and pleasures that I miss so much. Every glance of mine that fell on the two people I hold dearest would be worth a million other trivial pleasures. To be with the ones you love, to be well and happy, to be able to lift up your eyes to God with prayer and Thanksgiving are the things that really mean happiness. I would give anything to be able to take you in my arms and hold you close to me. I am more in love with you than ever before. I pray that next year we may be able to thank God that we are together again...

A cold, dismal rain drips steadily on American infantrymen slogging through the mud. Snow caps the high hills. On roadsides, in vineyards and olive groves of "sunny Italy", troops snatch much-needed rest. Punch-drunk with weariness, shoulders hunched against the chill wetness, they sit with their feet in the gumbo. Hot coffee is a Waldorf luxury... A soldier needs three blankets against the cold and rain. But he cannot carry them and fight too. A platoon leaves its rolls to be picked up by trucks. But trucks are hard to get, and they have a hard time reaching the platoon by night... This is a war of marching and fighting, more marching and more fighting...
~ Time, Nov 29, 1943

Nov 30, 1943
Bob in Italy to Daisy

I have received four Christmas boxes from you, and one each from our relatives. Thank you so much... It's difficult to write often, as we are busy as hell...

Dec 11, 1943

The height of my ambition is to be with you and make you happy... My outfit is doing a good job and you will be proud of me someday...

Dec 12, 1943

I have been in the mountains and couldn't write much. I grew quite a beard... Tell my daughter to save some of those kisses for me... Darling, I am awful lonesome for you these last few days. I hated being away from you on our anniversary. I lay up on a hill in a foxhole most of the day wishing I were back in your arms. I remember well that day three years ago. The rush it was to get there in time to get married. I never will forget what a wonderful feeling it was to go to that hotel with you as my wife. I am lucky to have you and Nikki waiting for me...

Dec 13, 1943

I am saving the fruitcake and the candy for Christmas... I am with Eddy, Arnold and Frosty; I cook and they clean up... I'm in the thick of things, but we're holding up and it hasn't changed me...

Dec 17, 1943

I have been wet to the bone several times and haven't had a cold yet...

༶

Dec 18, 1943
John, St. Petersburg, FL to Daisy

Dearest Sister,

I'm glad that you have been hearing regular from Bob. Mail is the finest morale builder in the world... Mary had an operation, and I didn't find out until now, but she seems to be getting on fine. I hope she will go to Florida, lie in the sun and get well. Tell Mother not to worry about us, and Mary will tell you both about herself. Love—Your brother, John

Dec 18, 1943
Bob in Italy to Daisy

Hey My Dearest Darling,

I hit the jackpot on mail last night. Received 5 letters from you and one from Eleanor. The snapshots are really good to look at. Nikki is a pretty little girl. Seeing pictures of you and her really make me want to be with you. I get so dam tired of not seeing you, and not knowing when I will get to be with you. . . Tell the folks at home that my outfit is doing a good job in Italy.

Dec 19, 1943

I would love to spend tonight with you. . . Thank you for all the Christmas presents, especially the handy knife. . . I had a hot bath today for the first time in 47 days. I took time off to go back and see a show. . . Nikki is such a cute little tyke. I hope it's possible for her to have a brother. . .

Dec 20, 1943

I was kinda blue in the letter I wrote last night. I didn't mean to be, Darling. Quite often, I get kinda peeved at everything that keeps me from being with you, but I try not to be blue in my letters. I realize that you have a lot of trouble yourself keeping your morale up. Darling, I am still doing okay. . . I would give anything if I could know Nikki now. There is going to be so much difference in her when I get home that I won't know how to take her. Imagine leaving a baby and coming back to find a little girl. Tell her about her Daddy so she will know me when I get home. I love you...

Dec 21, 1943

If I could only get back to you, I would never complain about anything to you again... Our outfit is doing good work. We're in Time magazine Nov 15th and Nov 24th... We are not just laying around over here for nothing...

> *[In Sicily, two Chemical Warfare Service mortar platoons maintained a smoke screen for 14 hours. Another unit switched to high explosive when attacked by Italian tanks, disabled three before the others retreated. Last month [in Italy], the 4. 2 automatic howitzer showed its usefulness at the crossing of the Volturo. One unit screened infantrymen as they slid down the bank, waded and swam to the German side of the river. Another outfit smoked up the area where Engineers were building a bridge under fire, kept them well screened until the job was done.*
> *~Time, November 15, 1943]*

Dec 23, 1943

I love you, Darling, and wish I could be with you on this eve of Christmas Eve. It is awful hard, Darling, for me to think of you and Nikki trying to enjoy Christmas without me being there to help you...

Dec 24, 1943

We got a bottle of Scotch, had a party and sang some carols... I'll love you anyway, but I'm hoping you won't get too fat so we can safely have our boy when I get home...

```
DEC 25, 1943 BOB TO DAISY
(TELEGRAM)
LOVE AND BEST WISHES FOR CHRISTMAS
AND THE NEW YEAR. ALL WELL.
```

Dec 25, 1943

I have enjoyed Christmas as much as I could; I thought of you constantly, and wanted to be at home with you and Nikki...

Please keep up your courage. I have a job to do over here and I think I can do a good one. Our outfit is tops in any man's language. I am so dam proud of my company that I hardly know what to do. They have proved themselves over and over again. Even tonight, with Christmas on the battlefield, the boys got together over the phone, and have been singing Christmas carols to each other for the last two hours...

Dec 29, 1943

I was thinking of you all day long on your birthday yesterday... I was up in the hills... I'm glad you liked the roses. I'm proud that Nikki's walking so soon and doing well...

Dec 31, 1943

Hey My Dearest Darling, It's New Year's Eve, and I wish I could be with you... I'm sitting here beside an open fire in a little Italian house. Once in a while, I can hear some of the sounds of war that is going on here. I wish it all was over, and I was back by your side once again. I feel so lonely tonight, Darling, that all I can do is turn my thoughts to God and to you. Those are the two most important things in my life right now. Over here, I couldn't ever get along without either one... I'm praying to return safe and sound. I feel close to you, and know that you are thinking of me... All my love forever, Bob

The Italian Campaign, from July 10, 1943 to May 2, 1945, was a series of Allied beach landings and land battles from Sicily and southern Italy up the Italian mainland toward Nazi Germany. The campaign seared into history the names of such places as Anzio, Salerno and Monte Cassino, as Allied armies severed the German-Italian Axis in fierce fighting. The Allied advance through Italy produced some of the most bitter, costly fighting of the war, much of it in treacherous mountain terrain. Among the British and American troops were Algerians, Indians, French, Moroccans, Poles, Canadians, New Zealanders, African and Japanese Americans.
-History.com

Staff, Italian Campaign, 2009.
The "Winter Line" of heavily fortified German positions, proved a major obstacle to the Allied advance. From early November to late December, the Fifth Army sustained 16,000 casualties. By the end of December, weather conditions included blizzards, drifting snow and zero visibility.

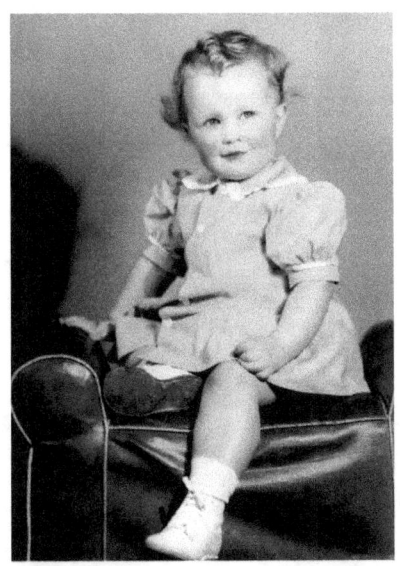
Nikki

Nikki and Daisy

Captain Robert A. Guy

VI. 1944—The Price of Freedom

I am looking forward to that day when I get off the train in Chester and rush to meet you...

Bob, Italy, January 1944

January 1, 1944
Bob in Italy to Miss Martha Carlson at Ciba, NYC

Dear Martha, I received your letter a few days ago and was glad to hear all the news. You never know how good the American way of life is until you see how the rest of the world lives. It seems like an awful long time since I left the company that morning in 1940. I hope it won't be long until I can drop in and say hello to all. I enjoyed the cigarettes and Reader's Digest subscription from Ciba Co. Keep me posted on how things are. Next to food, letters from home are one of the essentials over here.

Sincerely, Bob Guy

Jan 1, 1944
Bob to Daisy

I don't know when I have spent a quieter New Year's Eve. The only noise came from a few guns shooting and the wind howling around the house. Next year I am going to make up for this one, and celebrate with you. . . I don't have much to write about, but I think about you day after day. How did Nikki enjoy her Christmas? It must be fun to watch one of your own enjoy life and express herself. . .

Jan 3, 1944

I have received 8 V-mails from you. I enjoyed every word of them, Darling. Our mail comes in spots but I think it will be better now that Christmas is over. Tell that Daughter of mine not to get too spoiled for her daddy will straighten her out when he gets home, ha, ha. Wish I could be there. We have had quite a few promotions lately. Anscombe made Captain, and a bunch of others made 1st Lts. Eddy and the chaplain are due for Captain. We just received the news. Audrey had a boy and Alma had a girl. Johnny had a quart of whiskey bet on each baby. George lost twice. Imagine that—betting on your baby. Darling, I love you. Wish I could hold you in my arms tonight.

All my love forever, Bob

> *

Jan 5, 1944
Daisy to Bob in Italy

Dearest Darling,

Received two letters from you—dated Dec. 34 and 31st. That's pretty quick. Darling, I do miss you an awful lot, but as long as I know you're all right, I can stand it. Please don't get careless. I love you with all my heart and always will; I want you so bad. It's been such a long time, hasn't it? Frances W. said a Captain called her, and said that he was next to Harry M. in a Hospital over there, and that Harry's getting along fine but couldn't tell her anything else. She keeps saying, "Don't you think they'll send him home" and I keep saying, "Why of course," when she knows good and well that I don't know a dam thing about it, but it always helps to get a little encouragement. Nikki and Jesse, her nurse, are playing all over the place. Nikki makes us lift her up and tell her about every picture, and then she exclaims over them. She cares nothing for dolls but loves books and turns pages as if she were 10 years old. She still likes that little stuffed dog you had for her when we arrived in El Paso. I hope she won't be a "Quiz kid!" Wouldn't that be terrible! Darling, I wish you could be here with us and pray it won't be so terribly much longer. I'm so glad you can sit by a fire once in a while, and I'm so glad you're proud of your men. I'm proud of you, Darling.

All My Love Always, Daisy

Jan 5, 1944
Bob to Daisy

Hey My Dearest Darling,

I am holding up remarkably well, considering all the bad weather. We are fixed up real well on clothes. When I have to go out in the rain or snow, I can keep warm and dry. I am trying to write almost every day, so you will get lots of letters with lots of love. I can't let you forget me. Maybe if I write you a lot you will let me kiss you when I get home. . . George bet Johnny that Alma would have a boy and Johnny bet him that Audrey would have a boy. Poor George lost both ways and now he is in for 2 quarts of whiskey. I told them not to let Alma & Audrey hear about those bets. Tell me the details when you find out. Did Audrey come out okay? I love you lots & lots, loads & loads and heaps & heaps. Remember that expression? It comes, as near as anything, to expressing that my whole life is wrapped up in you. There are so many things we will have to catch up on. . . What are we going to do with Nikki at night when I get home? Let her sleep with your mother. Isn't it funny to think about little things like that? Are you blushing Daisy?

P. S. Please send Airmail envelopes & thin paper

Jan 5, 1944

Darling, I wish I could be with you just for a little while. It has been a long time... I am looking forward to getting a bunch of letters from you. I can hardly find anything to write about tonight except that I love you and want you real bad. How is Nikki? You say she is smart. I hope so. I would like to see her. I hate to have her grow up without knowing her daddy...

PS. Please send me some chocolate candy if you can.

Jan 8, 1944

We are going to get a much-needed rest after two months on the line. I had a real good beard... What color hair is Nikki going to have? I hope it will have a touch of red. That would be real pretty. I hope we can get her a good life, and some brothers and sisters... Tell Kirk I am still interested in farming... I love you a thousand times more since being in the war...

Jan 10, 1944

For the first time in months, I am able to take it easy, relax, and get some rest. I am on a five-day pass in a rest camp and it really is swell. I have a room by myself in a hotel... How I wish you could be with me tonight... I saw my first show since we left Sicily. It was "Stage Door Canteen"...

Jan 12, 1944
Daisy to Bob

Dearest Darling,

I went to the hospital to have my wisdom teeth out. I didn't want to tell you and worry you. I cried when coming out of the ether, about you, about Nikki being all right, about my "cigs" not being there. After I woke up, I read a letter from you dated Dec. 18. Darling, I'm glad you're doing alright, but listen, be careful. I'd rather have you back than any medals. Nikki came over twice to the hospital to see me and had a wonderful time. She'd forgotten all about me...

Jan 12, 1944
Bob to Daisy

How are you today, Darling? I am really enjoying my rest. It is such fun to sleep in a good bed, sit in soft chairs, and eat from a table with plates and stuff.

It does make me miss you a lot more, though. Every night when I go to my room, I miss you and want you there with me. I haven't been doing much sightseeing so far. Just laying around and taking it easy... I think it's alright if I tell you I am staying on the Isle of Capri. Some place. I can see that it has quite an attraction to tourists. Darling, I hope it won't be too long now until I can be with you again. I need you to help me forget all about this war...

Jan 13, 1944
Daisy to Bob

Dearest Darling, Received your letters of Dec. 21 & 24 today, and was so glad to get them. I really had to laugh about the part of not getting too fat. I'm off a good 15 lbs. after the "bout" with my wisdom teeth! Same ole Bob! I'll do my best not to gain it back. You seem sort of worried that we won't have a "boy" next time. Personally, I'll take what I can have and be thankful if all our children are girls. It makes me feel bad when you keep saying you'd like a boy next time, when I'm terribly proud of Nikki and no other child can ever take her place in my heart. Do you feel that way because there are so many boy babies in the Battalion, or what? So glad you all were able to get a quart of scotch for New Year's Eve. Darling, I do hope we won't be separated another Christmas. I think the war with Germany will be over by then.

Alice Love wrote me that Frosty sent her a medal that Mussolini issued to Mothers of 7 children. Frosty signed the note to her—"Yours hopefully and with high ambitions". . . I can just see Alice laughing! Hope you're taking good care of yourself. I'll try not to take in any extra poundage for your sake.

All My Love Always, Daisy

Jan 14, 1944

Dearest Darling,

Enjoyed the v-mails from you today so much. I'm glad you all had some Christmas spirit. I hate to think of what you are going through over there. It must be horrible. I'm so thankful every time I hear that you're getting along alright. Dr. ____ said I was getting along fine. He said I had the two worst embedded wisdom teeth he'd ever seen. I feel 100% better except I can't eat a thing solid yet, so maybe I'll get real skinny. Wouldn't you like that? Isabel came to see me in the hospital; she and Charley go over every night to their house and work on it. He's put in new floors and is going to build cabinets in the kitchen. I told her to fix up a bedroom in grand style for Nikki and me to spend a week or two in the country this summer. I feel terrible every time I think of Daddy's death 'cause I know he'd have loved Nikki so much, and she'd have had such a good time staying in the country...

Date uncertain, Jan, 1944
Bob to Daisy

Hey My Dearest Darling,

The Battalion is back for a rest now and it is about time for we have been in the line constantly since November. I am well and real glad to get that campaign over without injury to myself, for it was a particularly hard one. I lost a little weight, but outside of that, I am feeling fine. We are staying in a little town now and in a house again. It is really pleasant to sit back, relax, and not have to worry about anything for awhile... The Third has an excellent record so far, and you can be dam proud when you tell anyone that your husband is in the Third. We hope to have at least one unit decoration soon, so there won't be any doubt as to how good we are. Our battalion has had a tough time in the two years since it has been activated, but it has turned out to be really good. Make sure you understand that I am okay. Don't mention anything to the girls until you hear something from them, for just before we pulled out of the lines, we had a pretty hard blow. I can't tell you about it, but want you to be sure that I am okay when you hear something. I am sorry I can't explain it, but I had to warn you to look out for some bad news. This is a tough war, no doubt about it. I am glad I put in the time I did in preparing myself. Darling, you shouldn't think that you are not doing anything for this war. You have been doing an excellent job in sticking by me. Your letters are all that a man could ask for, and knowing that you and Nikki are waiting for me makes this life bearable. Anything I do is half yours, because without your help I don't know whether I could stand it. Keep up your spirits, keep writing me, and you will be doing more good than you realize. When I get a chance to look in your eyes and hold you in my arms again, you will know how deep my love is for you. It was nine months yesterday since I left you, and my love for you has grown nine million times. I don't see how I existed before I fell in love with you. . . Your last letters were real treats. They were nice and long and newsy. Every boy from home must be overseas now from the number of waiting wives you talk about. Write me lots about Nikki, and what she does. How is your mother?

All my love forever, Bob

Not dated, Jan, 1944

Hey My Dearest Darling,

I am enjoying relaxing after the last couple of months. It hasn't rained since we have been here and that is a pleasure. Erwin, Endsley, Clarke, two other officers & myself are staying in a room that an Italian family let us use. We are trying to give everyone a chance to take it easy, and get a new hold on everything. It takes a lot out of a man to stay at the front as long as we did, and you certainly need a rest such as this. We never know when we will be going back and we want to be ready for it when it comes. I went to church this morning and really enjoyed it. I get a lot more out of going to church over here. I will never again take religion as matter-of-factly as I used to. When the chips are down, you have to have someone to believe in. Daisy, in a tight spot, I always think of God and pray that it will be his will for me to come back to you. Darling, I feel sure that I will see you this year. This thing over here is so immense, but I don't see how the Germans can stand up very much longer. I am looking forward to that day when I get off the train in Chester and rush to meet you, and make you forget all those lonely months that we have been apart. I am always thinking of you, Darling, and wishing I could be there. Even though I miss you like hell, and want to be with you so dam bad it hurts, I hardly ever feel blue and discouraged for I realize that it is a worthy cause to be able to fight for the kind of life that we have. I don't believe that anywhere in the world can you get as much out of life as we do in the States. When I see these people over here and how they live, I am so dam thankful that Nikki is an American and will have the opportunity to live as Americans do. Daisy, every letter you write tells me that you believe in things as I do. I know it was awful hard on you to see me spending more time on the Army and neglecting you, but you were wonderful about it all along. You went through innumerable inconveniences and always stood by me even when we didn't have money enough to live on. I never will forget how wonderful you have been about the Army having more of me than you had. Daisy, you have given me the fullest three years of my life, and beautiful memories that I carry with me in my heart...

Not dated, Jan, 1944

Some of the worst nights of this war, I have spent in a foxhole in constant danger, but still at peace. When I think of you and Nikki, I know that it is worth it. Darling, I have never spoken about this to you before because I feel that I will come back, but if it is God's will that I will be taken over here, I want you to go on living for Nikki. Don't give up, for I wouldn't want that. You know that I love you, and all we can do is to put our trust in God and hope that he will see fit to bring us together again. Daisy, I hope you don't mind me saying this. I didn't want to worry you for I am perfectly alright, but just had to write you from the bottom of my heart. . .

Some bad news is coming; don't want to say anything about it now. . . I appreciate your letters; they make my life bearable. . . I want to get a hot shower this afternoon. Wish I could bathe with you in the tub like we used to. Would you like that? Give Nikki a hug for me and tell her she had better be good until her daddy comes home. . .

Jan 15, 1944

I'm back with the outfit and enjoyed the rest. I have received 4 letters, a V-mail, and snapshots of Nikki. She is getting to be a cute girl. Wish I could see her. . . You have been doing a swell job of writing. Mail from you keeps my spirits up and that is what we need over here. It will soon be a year now since I left you that day at Alice Love's. Wish all this would end soon and let me get back. A man can stand just so much. Don't ever forget that I love you with all my heart and always will.

Jan 17, 1944

How are your finances? I hope you have enough to live on. I know Nikki costs a lot to keep up, but as long as you can live comfortably on what you get, then I don't worry. You don't mind the war bond each month, do you? I never had any money to go to school on and I want to start now, saving something for our kids to go to school on when they grow up. . . Tell everyone at home hello for me. . .

On January 17, 1944, the Allied invasion of Cassino, in central Italy, was launched. The ancient town, near the Rapido River, was a strategic point in the Gustav line, a German defensive front. Despite Allied air superiority, it took four grueling battles over several months to break through heavily fortified Monte Cassino, an ancient Benedictine Abbey on a 1700 ft. rock high above the town.
~History. com

Jan 17, 1944
Daisy to Bob in Italy

I feel 100% better than I did last Monday when I had my wisdom teeth out. I even walked down to the Post Office last night to see if I got a letter from you. . . Mamie and R. C. came by to see me yesterday. Nikki really showed off for them. Laughed and carried on as if she sees them every day. Darling, I'm so glad you haven't had a cold. Please don't get careless. I guess my letters sound right foolish always asking you to take care of yourself, but Darling, I do mean it as you mean everything in the world to me and always will. . . It's been nine months since I last saw you and it seems more like nine years. Received the war Bond and will put it in the bank with the rest. Nikki didn't take a nap yesterday. When I was feeding her supper, she went to sleep in her high chair. She plays so hard during the day. Darling, I love you loads and loads...

All My love, Daisy

Jan 18, 1944
Bob to Daisy

Hey My Dearest Darling, Each day brings me closer to you... I drove 20 miles tonight with Ross and John to see "Above Suspicion." Although good, it wasn't worth the long trip. Do you go to the show much now? It is so nice and quiet up here where we are now. We are in a little town that is far off the main track... I love you Darling

Jan 27, 1944

Daisy,

I am sending you a scarf with your picture painted on it. I had it done by an artist while I was in rest camp. It is pretty good and I thought you would like it. Tell Nikki hello for me...

January 29, 1944

Hey My Dearest Darling,

We are taking it easy. It is a beautiful night. I was outside a little while ago, and stayed by myself, trying to get as close to you as possible. Those are the times when I can almost feel you there beside me. The air was completely still, not a cloud moved the beauty of millions of stars. I could see the reflection of the new moon, which had just gone down behind the top of a mountain, and I thought of how much I loved you, and of having you by my side on just such a night, thanking God that we are together again. But, even then, there was the constant reminder of this war. I could see flashes and hear the rumble of the big guns up at the front. You can never quite forget that there is a war going on while you are here. Still I was unafraid, standing there in the night, feeling you close to me and knowing that you are thinking of, and loving me. I get all the courage I need to do my job. It is amazing how much actual comfort I get just thinking of you. I will never forget the afternoon I came back from Florida in a G. I. truck. I saw you through the door of that cute house we had in Predios. The next time will be more wonderful than that. Oh Darling, I have so many beautiful memories to keep me company until I get home. Remember the afternoon we spent in bathing suits in the pasture, back of our house (don't blush Darling), or the weekend we had at Clemson, the trip up to that cabin on the lake, the mill pond and the moon in the trees, our other favorite parking place, or our first blind date? Even that was a big success. I will never forget how good I felt when you walked down the walk at the Darby's, holding on to my arm. . . By the way Darling, I am real proud of Nikki. I think she is going to be a beauty. I certainly would like to be with her. Nine months brings about quite a change. I won't know how to get along with her at first. It was exactly nine months ago today that I sailed from New York. It seems like years. . . Daisy, you really must not worry about me. It doesn't do any good. Put your faith in God, be strong. Take good care of yourself and Nikki and I will be back with you before you know it.

All my love forever to my darling wife and daughter, Bob

Jan 29, 1944
Daisy to Bob

Dearest Darling,

Kirk called me tonight to tell me about Harry Raysor. When I got through talking to him, I was shaking like a leaf and I hadn't heard from you since the first of the week... So I ran the whole way to the Post Office, and got two V-mails from you, dated Jan. 10. Bob, I was so terribly thankful to hear from you, I hardly knew what to do, so I just cried. I felt like such a dam fool, with my hair all curled up—got a new p. wave this morning, and you fighting somewhere. It knocked the props out from under me hearing about Harry. I'll be so glad when this war is won and you can come home to me. Never forget, I'll always love you with all my heart forever and ever. Bob, Nikki means so much to me. If I didn't have her, I don't know what I'd do. Thank you so much, Darling... I'm so glad you got to rest in such a nice place... I hope you are still there.

All My Love Always, Daisy

Probable date, Jan 31, 1944

I love you so terribly much and hope you're alright. I can't breathe easy 'til you're back at home with me. Please take as good care of yourself as you can. I was so excited to get two letters from you last night that I didn't settle down to what you had to say 'til after the tenth reading today! Glad you got a five-day pass and had a good bed to sleep in. I'd give anything if I could have been with you those five days. I wouldn't have let you sleep a minute, much less rest!! Darling, I'm building all my hopes on when you come home for good and we'll forget this awful separation. I'm going to try so hard to make you forget what you've been through. Bob, Kirk called last night about Harry; the Raysors called him. I sent Melba a telegram this morning and wrote her tonight. I hope from the bottom of my heart that it is the last letter of that kind I'll write during this war. Everything I said seemed so useless. If you have time, wish you'd write either Melba or the Raysors. Alice and Mr. Guy took me over to see the home guard drill, then, came by here. Mr. Guy spent the afternoon playing with Nikki. She loved playing with his car keys, and rolling a ball back and forth between them sitting on the floor!

February 2, 1944
Bob to Daisy

Hey My Dearest Darling,

I am enjoying the pictures of Nikki—I like the one taken at the Darbys' and the expression on her face. I want more close-ups of both of you together. . . I'm sorry you were in the hospital. Please tell me when you're sick. . . I'm sending three cameos to have mounted as you want. . . I'm hurting because I haven't seen you for so long. Give my love to Nikki.

February 5, 1944

Your letter of Jan 17 came in yesterday and I sure enjoyed it. Your letters help so much. Don't worry about me for I am going to take care of myself. . . I guess _____ isn't in the army due to helping run the farm. Darling, after seeing what it is like over here, you can't help but feel a little mad at the ones who stay behind. I'll file the income tax when I get back. . . . I would like some home life in the States now. Over here, you long for the time when you can be home again with your loved ones. You go on day after day, with nothing worth looking forward to except that trip home, and nothing worth looking back on except the wonderful time you had before you left. . . . When I listen to music, I want to dance with you. . . . We had fun together in El Paso. . . Erwin has never seen his baby.

Give my love to Nikki. All my love forever, Bob

Feb. 9, 1944
(postmarked March 9)

Hey My Dearest Darling,

I am trying to write as often as possible so there won't be a break in my letters even though the conditions are not very good for writing. I am being as careful as I possibly can. Everything is still the same. No news except war news and I don't like to write about that. Daisy, I am not set upon having a boy next. I am always so dam glad when anything goes well that it doesn't matter. My only hope is that I will get back to you safe and sound. That is the only big worry right now. I feel the same as you do—no other child will ever replace any of the affection I hold for Nikki. Wish I could see her now. I hope you can read this letter. I am writing in a foxhole and it is hard to write plain. . . . I love you Darling and always will.

Feb. 14, 1944

My Darling Daisy & Nikki,

I have already written you once this morning but was so

dam cold I could hardly write. Then your letter came in saying you had heard about Harry. I tried to write, so you would not be worried about it, but you heard before my letters got there. That thing was an awful blow to us over here, but there was nothing to do but to take it. I hope you will extend my sympathies to Harry's family and tell them that I cannot write any of the details. You will probably hear from the others concerned by the time you get this letter. I don't dare write who else was in this because it would be censored but I can say Johnny, Frosty, Erwin, Ross, Fallwell, Morse, Fenton, Wales, Ramsey and Eddy are still okay. I hope this letter goes through okay, for they are awful hard on their censoring. Darling, I am still doing my share in the fight over here and if God is willing, have every intention of coming back to you real soon. Don't worry Daisy, put your faith in God for he is the only one who can keep you believing in the right things. I love you Darling.

All my love to my wife and baby, Bob

Feb 15, 1944

Dearest Darling & Nikki,

I hope you are not worrying yourself sick since you heard about Harry for it won't do any good. I will be in danger as long as I am over here and there's nothing we can do except trust in God. I am very eagerly looking forward to the time when I will be warm again. I am very tired of this cold weather. Thank Goodness most of the winter has already gone. Daisy, I hope you understand how hard it is to write at all while we are in the lines. I wouldn't try to write at all but I know even though these are not good letters you will glad to just hear from me. How is Nikki? I will be looking for some more pictures of her real soon. It really helps when I get pictures of you and Nikki. Have one taken with that new permanent of yours. I would like to see it. Darling you shouldn't feel bad about that. I don't want you to give up everything. I am giving enough for both of us. Daisy, I wish I could tell you how much I long to be at home with you and Nikki. It is really awful. I love you with all my heart and always will.

All my love forever, Bob

Feb 12 or 17, 1944

Hey My Dearest Darling,

I received your airmail letter of January 31 today Darling. It was certainly a nice letter. I have been sweating out your next few letters for I am worried about your reaction to all the bad news. If I could only be with you at times like that, it would be better. I hate for you to have to stand all that by yourself. Daisy, I am taking care of myself and not taking any more chances than necessary. After all, over here the only real thing that I want is to do my job and get back to you safely. I enjoyed that part in your letter talking about Daddy playing all afternoon with Nikki. Sure wish I could be at home doing the same thing. Daisy, I really long for some of that good ole Chester life. It would certainly be a wonderful feeling to step down from that train in Chester and be in your arms again. I think of that day so much that I am sure it will have to come soon. Darling, I will write a letter to Harry's folks and tell them as much as I can. I love you Daisy and feel so proud of you and Nikki. Keep up your good work Darling, I'll be back soon.

All my love forever, Bob

On February 15, 1944, Allied bombers obliterated the monastery Monte Cassino. This tactical error, due to a mistranslation of intelligence, made the site a better observation post for the German army. Allied control of the area and the fortified town of Cassino, was not won until May 18, 1944.

Monte Cassino, restored in the 1950's, is a shrine for relatives of the estimated 183,000 soldiers on all sides who lost their lives in the battles around it.

~John Ezard, The Guardian, April 3, 2000

Robert Adams Guy was killed during the battle for Monte Cassino on February 17, 1944. Daisy kept writing to him, until March, when she was notified of his death. The following letters were later returned to her, unopened.

Jan 18, 1944
[*Returned to sender, marked "Deceased," Mar 21, 1944*]

Dearest Darling, I am sending airmail paper. I told the dentist that Nikki's front teeth are right far apart; he said that yours were the same way... Darling, I do hope you and your men are all right. I'm fine, but feel as if I've been on every foot of ground leading to Rome. It's been such a terrible struggle hasn't it? I listen to just about every news broadcast, and am so glad whenever a mile is gained. Nikki and I went to see Lillian B. and her little girl. Nikki had the time of her life, as little Lillian is just Nikki's size although she's a whole year older... I love you and am waiting for you...

Jan 20, 1944

[Returned unopened March 21, 1944]

Do you want candy and stamps? I'm so glad you all have plenty of warm clothes and can keep dry. I'd love to have a date with you next New Year's Eve. You should see Nikki—she's sitting on her "pot" and has the hiccups! She discovered a while back that she can get up by herself so sometimes she walks right off without any pants on. Soon I'm going to put training pants on her. They're just little bloomers, but it breaks them from wetting their pants quicker than anything! I'm always glad when I hear from you saying you're all right and that you love me. Please take care of yourself.

Lots of Love Always, Daisy

Jan 20, 1944

[Airmail papers enclosed. Returned to Sender unopened May 4, 1944]

Dearest Darling, I wish I could put my arms around you, hold you close, and just forget this whole struggle. When the war is won, we can begin all over again. You wrote that you were in need of some loving -well I'm ready, willing and able! Bob, I feel so good since I had those wisdom teeth out. Darling, our daughter is such a funny little person. Gets awful mad when I pick her up just to hold her! She wants to walk and run everywhere without any assistance. If you say "Dance, Nikki" she stamps her feet and laughs at the top of her voice. When you come home and see her, you'll love her so much. After you're with her a while, you'll feel that you haven't been away so long after all. Julia said her husband will soon be overseas two years. They were married about three weeks when he left. I'm so glad we had so much more time. . .

Jan 31, 1944

[Airmail papers enclosed. Returned unopened March 21, 1944]

Received your Jan 17 letter this morning; it was such a nice long one and I've enjoyed reading it over and over... I got your box off this afternoon with airmail and candy... I enjoy sending things to you. Nikki is so terribly independent and wants her own way all the time, but she's so sweet and cute with it all. When I give her a cracker, she offers to give everyone in the room a bite and if anyone has anything to eat and doesn't give her a bite, she fusses in baby talk at the top of her voice. She can say Bob, ball, boy, man, bye, Meow, and Moo like a cow! Isn't she smart!

Feb 1, 1944

[Returned May, 1944]

Dearest Darling,

Well here it is another month closer 'til you can come home, and I hope and pray it won't be as long as it has been. Keep letting me know you're alright... I framed the 10 roses you sent on our anniversary. Nikki's getting along just wonderful, and so am I, so don't worry about us...

Feb 2, 1944

[Returned Mar 21, 1944]

I am doing fine with the money, and don't want you to go without, since you're giving up enough as it is...

Feb 6, 1944

[Returned Mar 21]

Nikki is staying with Kirk and having the time of her life with all those kids and the dog. Patti has taken complete charge of her and little Kirk wants to know why Nikki can't read to him! Nikki thinks she's every bit as big as Patti and has to do everything they do! I love you with all my heart. Please take care of yourself. The fighting in Italy must be really awful from what I read and hear on the radio... I'll be so thankful when you are home. I'd give anything if I could wake up in the middle of the night and find your arms around me. It's been such a long time, hasn't it?

Feb 7, 1944
[Returned March 21]

Harriet took us uptown this morning, and I bought Nikki a pair of shoes. I called Melba today, but she was out of town with relatives. Her mother wanted to know if you knew details of Harry's death... Patti and little Kirk are showing Nikki off to all the kids in the neighborhood, and she loves it... I pray you're alright...

Feb 9, 1944
[Returned March 21]

I got your V-mail of Jan 21... I love you more and more each day... The Raysors are upset and want more news... I'm sorry for forgetting Valentine's Day... I like the jewelry you sent me...

Feb 10, 1944
[Returned March 21]

I'm glad I don't have to live over these past months again... I have high hopes that you'll be home by the end of 1944... Elsie G. says she will go crazy if her husband is gone much longer, and she's by herself with the children. I do hope you're still resting...

Will you write Mr. Raysor as soon as you get a chance, and tell any details of Harry's death?

All My Love Always, Daisy

> Feb 15, 1944
> [Returned March 21, 1944]

I enjoyed your mail of Jan 27... Nikki helps me by being a part of both of us; she gives me something to hang on to while you're away. I try to be as contented as possible... Harriet says Nikki is fat, but pretty... We'll have Nikki with us a year longer as the schools in S. C. have added a twelfth grade!

> Feb 19, 1944
> [Returned May 25, 1944; "Deceased and undeliverable"]

Received a long letter from Audrey. Two days after she got my letter about Harry, she received a letter from Alma saying George was also killed Jan. 12. It's just all too awful to be true. She also said Frosty is in charge now so does that mean Stark died too? Write what you can and please take care of yourself... I love you with all my heart and will forever and ever. Audrey's labor was easy. She sent pictures. Tell Johnny he has a cute little ole boy...

> Feb 20, 1944
> [Returned unopened May 4, 1944]

Haven't heard from you since the last letter, Jan. 27. It must have been an awful blow to the Battalion to lose those boys, and knowing them so well. Don't let those awful things get you down, as one doesn't go until his time comes, no matter what, or more people would be killed in this war... I told you a while back that

_____ was going to be drafted. His number came up and the people got up a petition saying he was the church Superintendent, on the school board, and his grandmother depended on him, so they deferred him indefinitely! Your daughter upset a bowl of flour all over her a while ago. She's into everything now and won't sit still a minute... _____ was sick in Fla. with spinal meningitis, but they gave him the new drug that starts with a P. and he's getting along fine. There were two cases of it at Pryor Hospital. They got the drug and went home cured. Isn't that wonderful?

I miss you so much. It seems years since I told you good-bye in El Paso. This is the longest winter I've ever spent, yet we've so much to be thankful for. I just keep looking ahead to the time when you come home, and we'll be young enough to start all over again... Darling, you ought to get this about the time you're 26 years old and I wish I could be with you. Next year, we'll make it a real birthday.

All My Love Always, Daisy

Feb 22, 1944
[Returned May 8]

I got your airmail of Feb 5. I love and want you, with a longing that goes on and on... All day today, Mary and I were serving and talking to the soldiers that just got in from maneuvers... Bob, I'm so glad to do anything along that line for those boys and hope someone will do it for you... A friend of mine has a date with a married soldier, and wanted me to go along. What do all these girls think they are doing? I always thought one would go straight to hell... When I can't have you, there isn't anyone else in the world for me...

March 3, 1944
[*Returned May 8*]

I had a good time at "The Service Wives League"... No mail at the Post office today. I wish I could still think you're in a rest area, but somehow feel you're back at the front. I hate to even think of what you're going through... If I didn't have Nikki, I would have joined the WAC's as soon as you left. 'Course I'm awful glad I've got her, but I feel like a slacker with some girls doing so much. I really would like to go overseas...

March 3, 1944
[*Returned May 8*]

Hey My Dearest Darling,

Did you ever receive the box I sent you in Jan.?

At our next meeting of the "Wives Service League," we are going to bring our souvenirs. I'm going to take Nikki's and my Christmas presents; I hope my cameos come soon. Several of the girls have grass skirts from the South Pacific... I do wish you could see Nikki; she's the busiest little thing you ever saw. If Mother or I do something she doesn't like, she shakes her head, and says "No, No, No!" I miss you so much at night, and on Sundays, as I always looked forward to you being home for Supper... So, I write to you and hope and pray you'll soon be home with me every night...

March 5, 1944
[Returned May 8, 1944, "Deceased"]

Dearest Darling,

Louise and I walked down to the Post Office tonight, and I got two V-mails from you dated Feb 15 & 17. I was so glad to get them. I know it's terrible for you to write, so I don't expect to hear so often while you're at the front. I know you're under an awful strain and must be fed up with not knowing when you can come home. Your letters are cheerful, Darling, but I can feel how you must be feeling... I'm not worrying myself sick over all the bad news, but the rest of my life and Nikki's depend on your coming home to us... I feel so sorry for Alma... My main thoughts are for your safety and our future above everything else. I'm doing my best to take what comes and trying not to let things get me down as they used to do. I feel terrible when I think about what you, and all the other boys, are giving up, but also realize that there is no way out but to fight and win this war. I'm so thankful that Nikki and I went to El Paso, and had those months together before you left. After you come back and are home for a week or two, Nikki will take right up with you and you won't feel like you've been away so long. She wouldn't have a thing to do with Kirk for the first few days when we were in Greenville, then she bothered the life out of him demanding to be picked up and wanted to sit in his lap all the time... I'm more than ready to take up with you! You won't have to push your affections on me. Your daughter has started wearing a bow in her hair. The way I work it is like this—she sits in my lap and I brush her hair real good and don't let her see the bow. I tie it in the top of her hair while she isn't looking! It's hard to fool her but I'm still trying! Bob, I love you with all my heart and always will forever and ever,

March 9, 1944
[*Returned unopened*]

Dearest Darling Bob,

　I hope you're getting along alright although I know the weather and everything is pretty awful over there. Darling, I wish I could tell you how many times every day I think about you—I'm conscious every min. of you being in danger, and not being able to help in any way. I'm sure you're coming back to me, and don't have the slightest doubt. That keeps me as contented as I'll ever be without you. I have so many hopes for us. . . Nikki's been a comfort. Don't know what I'd do without her. Her newest trick is to grab her coat and hat, run to the front door and say "Bye, Bye. " She loves to stay out in the fresh air and fusses when she is brought in. She's beginning to take a big interest in her dolls now—hugs and kisses them and rocks them in her little chair. She's a funny little girl when she laughs and rocks back and forth. I played bridge today with some friends, who are very pregnant. I hope I didn't look as bad as they do. . . Kirk stopped by, and was asking about you. . . Did you ever get the box? Darling, I love you loads & loads & heaps and heaps & lots & lots, and don't have to tell you that I want you, 'cause it's been a long time, hasn't it? All my love always, Daisy

---

MARCH 10, 1944
THE ADJUTANT GENERAL IN WASHINGTON, DC TO DAISY
THE SECRETARY OF WAR DESIRES ME TO EXPRESS HIS DEEP REGRET THAT YOUR HUSBAND CAPTAIN ROBERT A GUY WAS

KILLED IN ACTION IN DEFENSE OF HIS
COUNTRY ON SEVENTEEN FEBRUARY IN
ITALY PERIOD LETTER FOLLOWS

My grandmother and her neighbor, Mrs. Jackson, woke Mother up early on the morning of March 11, 1944, to give her the telegram that Bob was dead. We were told later that Daisy stayed in bed, grief-stricken, for about two weeks before she got up and went on with her life. I was 16 months old, and have no recollection of him, or that day. My first childhood memory is when I was four. Years later, after a death in the family, my sister and I woke Mother up early one morning. She then had a painful flashback of that terrible day; I saw her pain, yet could not console her.

March 12, 1944
Maud Bingham to Daisy

Those of us who loved Robert have many memories of him. . . . I took three of the best students in 10th grade geometry to Rock Hill to stand a district test. I can remember so well looking through the glass in the door and seeing him in the back row toward the windows—a young boy in a clean cotton shirt, bending over the paper. He had a good mind and a sense of honor and loved the finer things.

March 15, 1944
Alma in W. Va. to Daisy

[Alma enclosed a funeral program for her husband, Lt. George Arner, Jr., killed in action in Italy, Jan 12, 1944.]

I shudder to think how many more families will get such news before this thing is over. When it comes to those we know and love, it is almost too much to bear... The French government sent their Croix de Guerre, with an explanation that George was attached to a French unit, and killed by enemy bombardment. Harry Raysor was given the same, so no doubt they were together... At least we can be thankful we have our little girls...

> March 20, 1944
> Audrey in Oregon to Daisy

I am crying over your note. Why do these things have to happen to our fine young men? You can be proud of a fine, brave man, who was liked by everybody...

> April 2, 1944
> Daisy to R. H. [*not mailed*]

Dear Robert,

I appreciate your lovely letter of sympathy, as I know you have so little time to call your own. Bob's death was not as much of a shock to me as one might think. For two months before I was notified, I knew that he wasn't coming back. In one letter, he told me there was a great possibility that he would not, that Nikki was my responsibility, and I couldn't let her down. The 3rd Chemical Battalion was at the front for two and a half months before they were pulled back for a rest, and then went back into action around the first of Feb. Every time I received a letter in Jan, from one of the wives, it told the sad news of losing another of our close friends. Seven of our closest died, including the Colonel, which, of course, doesn't help me one bit, but makes it harder to bear...

Date unknown, 1944
Daisy to Alma [*not mailed*]

How glad I was to hear from you as I am now going through a suffering that I never knew existed, and no one can help me but myself. I have to carry on for Nikki, when sometimes it seems impossible. You know all of this too well. I'm going to work, as soon as I can get everything managed, in some other place, as I can't stay here in this town where I've waited for Bob to come back all these months. The people here have been wonderful to me and done things for me I never expected. There have been so many war deaths here as elsewhere. On Feb 5, Bob wrote, "If I am taken over here, you must remember that you have to carry on for Nikki as she is dependent on you. " I believe he knew that he wasn't coming back, and I felt it also, but never really believed it in the bottom of my heart. I also received nice letters from many men who taught Bob in college. Alma, it looks as if the Third was ill fated or something. They've lost so many fine men. . .

Date unknown, 1944
John to Daisy

Well honey, one more week at sea. . . If I get my Army commission, I'll get a few days off, and Mary and I will be up to see you all. How is that beautiful baby of yours, honest she is my pet. . . It's tough to be away from you all. Have you gotten your chin up and resolved on what you are planning to do? Is Mother's leg any better? Well dear, just a short note to let you know I haven't forgotten you—Love & kisses—brother

April 8, 1944
Frosty in Italy

My Dear Daisy:

It is with a heavy heart and humility that I write this letter to you, trying in my small way to offer what help I can in this tragic loss. My loss is small compared to yours, but for the fact that Alice & my sons may find themselves in a like position, I would hesitate to try to console you in a situation that allows no consolation. Bob and I were good friends for a long time. During December and January, I was with him a great deal, eating, cooking, sleeping, talking, and planning our lives after the war with our families. What a shock his passing was to all the people of the Battalion. To me it was a great personal loss. I haven't written you sooner because I couldn't bear to think of the tragedy—and censorship regulations forbid direct correspondence except after 90 days, or until I was sure you had been informed. There is so little I can say that will help to ease the ache in your heart. However, I will say that Bob did not suffer. He was given a Christian burial. He is resting in a well-kept American Cemetery. Knowing Bob, if he had been given a choice of a way to leave this world, he went the way he would have chosen, fighting for the Home & Family he loved so dearly. Call on me at any time, for anything I can do.

Sincerely, Frosty (Major Forrest E. Love)

April 16, 1944
The Service Wives' League to Daisy

It is with regret that we accept your resignation as an active member of the Service Wives' League... In your new work, may

1944—The Price of Freedom

you find peace of mind and the comfort of doing useful work. . .
We express our willingness to help you in any way. . .

> Not dated, 1944
> Capt. Charles R. Endsley, Jr,
> Edgewood Arsenal, Md., to Daisy

I want to assure you that Bob's death was quick & painless. He & I were sitting on the ground, studying a map together with a view to some firing we would do on the following day. It was around 4 PM in the afternoon of Feb. 17. A few mortar shells had been coming in all afternoon & two shells came in pretty close. One was off to our flank about 100 yards, while the other hit behind us in the direction of some of the men in the company. I stood up and looked back in the direction of the men to see if anyone had been hit. Then I realized that the shell off to our right had thrown a fragment, which had hit Bob. He was conscious for only a few seconds & the only words he spoke were "Catch me, Ross. I'm falling." I would say that he was conscious only about 10 seconds after & was dead in a matter of two minutes. I immediately began to administer first aid with the help of one of the company first aid & sent a jeep for the battalion surgeon, who was only about a mile to our rear. However, Bob had passed on before he arrived about 5 minutes later, and he said that he could have done nothing to have prevented Bob's death. The fragment, which struck Bob on the left side just below his hip, was a large one & passed completely through, smashing the bony structure as it went. His body was intact, however, when sent back for burial. I don't think Bob ever realized that he had been hit. I am really glad if he had to go, that it was that way. Like most of us over there, he had a greater horror of coming home mangled up than of getting killed, and only hoped that, if we were hit hard, it would take us. Bob was the finest friend I have ever had and I never expect to have another to whom I feel as close. Not only was he a good friend, but was one of the finest company commanders I have ever known. Every member of his command had complete confidence in him as a leader. I can assure you that he holds a place in our memory for as long as we live... He was buried in the cemetery which contains his friends, the other officers of the Battalion we had lost prior to his death. It is well cared-for & also contains the American men lost in the attacks around Cassino.

Capt. Charles R. Endsley, Jr.
C. W. School, Edgewood Arsenal, Md.

May 18, 1944
Fred Schlapp, Asst. Secretary, Ciba Co. in NY to Daisy

The undersigned, having served in France in the first world war, is very interested to know that Bob was awarded the French Croix de Guerre with a bronze star, which unquestionably was well deserved. He was one of the very first of our "Ciba Boys" to go, and to those of us who knew him here, it is extremely regrettable that so fine a young man who had hardly begun to live, will not return to us to take up where he left off...

Date uncertain, 1944
Chaplain Bolding to Daisy

The loss of your precious husband and our dear friend was an awful shock to us. He was one of our favorite officers... and the most faithful company commander in attending church services... His integrity, his patience, his kindness and generosity toward his men made him both respected and beloved... He was so jolly and optimistic that it was a joy to be in his company...

May 18, 1944
Eleanor to Daisy

I'm glad the dress fit Nikki... A friend in Italy, who is with the grave registration outfit, visited Bob's grave and said a prayer there. It is a nice place and well cared-for...

June 16, 1944
Capt. Charles Ross Endsley
Camp Butner, NC, to Daisy

Lt. Fish and I were the first officers to make it back home. I have been unable to get gas for my car to come to Chester... I was very close to Bob, and feel a great loss. Please write to me if you want more details of his death... I want you to know that no one will ever fill his place in the company. He was the best-loved company commander that I have ever known. You can't imagine how we all felt when we realized he was gone. We had complete confidence in him as a leader and commander in combat... Bob never had to give orders. All we wanted to know was what he wanted done, and it was done. His leadership was an inspiring thing. He never seemed to have the slightest feeling of fear when he set out to do something he felt was his duty, or something that would help his men. It was a great privilege to have served with Bob. You can call on me at any time I can be of service to you in any matter...

During June and July, 1944, other Army wives sent notes of condolence to Daisy.

Oct 2, 1944
Capt Charles Ross Endsley to Reuben Cassels Guy, Sr.

My Dear Mr. Guy,

I am sure you have given up hope of hearing from me... My mail was delayed, and I just received about twenty letters: one from Daisy, one from Bob's stepmother, and others that were forwarded from Italy. Thank you for inviting me to visit, but I can only leave the post for 24 hours at a time...

Bob's death was quick and painless. He was conscious for only a few seconds after being hit by a mortar shell fragment, and the only words he spoke were, "Catch me, Ross, I'm falling. " The fragment went through his left side just below the hip. First aid was given and the battalion surgeon was there within five minutes, but nothing could be done. His body was intact when sent for burial. I don't think Bob ever realized he had been hit. He, like most of us over there, had a greater horror of coming home mangled up, than of getting killed, and only hoped that if we were hit hard, it would take us. Bob was the finest friend I have ever had and I never expect to have another to whom I feel as close. Every member of his command had complete confidence in him. He holds a place in our memories as long as we live. He is buried in the American cemetery along with a number of his friends and the American men lost in the attacks around Cassino.

Yours very truly, Ross Endsley

Army Colonel Charles Ross Endsley, Jr., [1912-1991] returned to his home state of Tennessee after the war. From 1948 -1956, he was superintendent of Tennessee Military institute, and president from 1956 until he retired in 1971.

~From a phone call to Ross Endsley III in Tennessee by Nikki.

[*Excerpts from a letter*] Aug 16, 2006
Ross Endsley III, in Tenn. to Nikki in Tulsa, OK

... My dad participated in a landing at Anzio, and it seems rather likely that Bob did too. Bob died at Cassino, which fell on May 18, 1944, and "D" Day was not until June 6th of that year.

I'm not sure why I have such a strong impression of Dad's experience at Cassino and his friendship with Bob Guy. He must have spoken to me about these things more than once.. . . The U S. Army first approached the town of Cassino in January 1944. The monastery there did not fall to the Allies until May 18th. . . The bombardment of the monastery at Cassino must have been an unforgettable event. My dad said that for three days it was impossible to sleep, because the ground shook continuously (probably began before mid- February). . . I'll admit that I've had some difficulties dealing with Bob Guy's death as I grew up. . . I attended military school, and was in ROTC at Vanderbilt, and on active duty for two years in the Army. Frequently during that time, my thoughts would go back to that hillside near Cassino. I wondered if I would be brave enough to give up my life in combat like Bob did. Thanks to the Lord,. . . I never served in combat.

I've had some thoughts relating to Bob Guy's story since deciding to contact you (again). My wife and I are Christians and attempt to live close to the Lord Jesus Christ. I am comforted by the thought that, if Bob trusted Christ for his salvation, then only seconds after saying (to Dad), "Ross, I'm falling," he landed in the arms of his loving Savior. I hope this thought is a comfort to you as well as it was to me... For my dad to have commented often enough (about) his friendship with Bob, it must have been very special... I always had the impression that Bob was a person that Dad could depend upon completely...

Sincerely,
Ross Endsley III

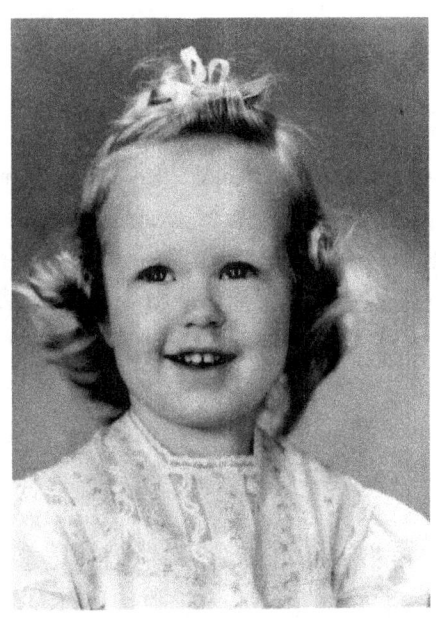

Daisy and Nikki with Harriet, Kirk and Patti

Epilogue

When I was about two years old, Mother moved us to live in Greenville with Kirk and Harriet. She worked as an X-ray technician at the hospital, where she met my future stepfather, a radiologist. They married when I was four. My brother was born when I was six; my sister, a year later.

We enjoyed life in a large colonial house in the country, had pretty clothes, good food, and took trips to the beach. My parents hosted friends at big parties and small dinners. Life was like the song, "Summertime." The living was easy; the cotton, high. Daddy was rich, and Mama, good-looking...

I was too young to remember my father Bob, the months of waiting for him to return, or his death. Mother told me, as I was growing up, that he died fighting in World War II. She said he knew, right away, that he would marry her. She often had vivid dreams that Bob came home to her. But, for her to talk about him in any detail was too emotional and upsetting. I only saw her cry once in our new home. She didn't share that Bob enjoyed the time with me in El Paso when I was a baby. I didn't know that he asked about me in almost every letter, valued my pictures, and always longed to see me again. Mother gave me the letter that he wrote to me for my first birthday. It was from Sicily, so I thought he died there.

My three paternal aunts came from out of state about once a year, and took me to lunch downtown at the Ottaray Hotel. When I visited my grandmother Daisy in Chester, Aunt Mamie and R.C. would have me out to their farm. I remember seeing my paternal grandfather Reuben once, at a distance.

As a Christian, and in my sixties, I began praying that I would meet someone who had known my father in the Army. A few months later, my daughter, who was living in France, phoned me with a question.

"What about grandfather?" she asked. She and her husband had visited the World War II memorial at Normandy. She was so moved by seeing all the graves, that she wanted to know where Bob had been in the war.

I asked Mother for more details, and found out that he died in Italy, during the battle for Monte Cassino. I wrote to Aunt Mamie in Chester; she sent photos and the letter from Ross Endsley. Bob's father had saved it for years. I realized how much his father had loved him.

Receiving my parents' letters has more than answered my prayers. I can understand my mother's pain and loss, which influenced her whole life. I am comforted that my 'Papa' did not suffer at the time of his death. My heart is healed to read, in his own words, that he loved me. I'm sure that I will know my father when I see him again in heaven, and it won't seem so long since we have been apart.

~Nikki Guy Latham

"The patriot's blood is the seed of freedom's tree."
~Thomas Campbell

"Soldier rest, thy warfare over."
~Sir Walter Scott

www.ingramcontent.com/pod-product-compliance
Lightning Source LLC
Chambersburg PA
CBHW071958290426
44109CB00018B/2064